MARGOT NORTHEY is a member of the faculty in Interdisciplinary Studies and English at Erindale College, University of Toronto.

Gothic elements in English-Canadian fiction have generally been regarded as idiosyncratic outcroppings, or, in French-Canadian novels, as a temporary phenomenon rather than as part of a recurring Canadian pattern. By analysing a number of Canadian works of fiction from the nineteenth century to the present, Margot Northey demonstrates that gothicism, in varying degrees and of various kinds, has been a continuing feature of our fiction. She uses 'gothic' to refer to a subjective view of the dark side of life, seen through the distorting mirror of the self with its submerged levels of psychic and spiritual experiences. The gothic is essentially symbolic in its approach and its mood is pre-eminently one of terror or horror. 'Grotesque,' frequently used in conjunction with 'gothic,' is taken as an aesthetic term, referring to a mode of writing emphasizing incongruity, disorder, and deformity. It arises from the juxtaposition or clash of the ideal with the real, the psychic with the physical, or the concrete with the symbolic. Detailed treatment is given to a limited number of works, some from the nineteenth century, some from the twentieth, and the focus is on varieties of gothic and grotesque fiction rather than on specific authors. *The Haunted Wilderness* is a fascinating and original contribution to Canadian comparative studies and to genre-oriented criticism.

MARGOT NORTHEY

The Haunted Wilderness: The Gothic and Grotesque in Canadian Fiction

UNIVERSITY OF TORONTO PRESS
Toronto and Buffalo

©University of Toronto Press 1976
Toronto and Buffalo
Printed in Canada

Library of Congress Cataloging in Publication Data

Northey, Margot.

    The haunted wilderness.
    Includes index.
    1. Canadian fiction – History and criticism. 2. French-Canadian fiction –
History and criticism. 3. Gothic revival (Literature) 4. Grotesque in literature.
I. Title.
PR9192.6.G74N6   811'.009   76-23329
ISBN 0-8020-5357-2
ISBN 0-8020-6296-2 pbk

Contents

Acknowledgements

I want to thank Professor Clara Thomas, who first introduced me to the study of Canadian literature at York University, and who, through the course of writing this book, offered advice, encouragement, and a title. I am also grateful to others who made helpful suggestions, especially to professors Robert Adolph and Thomas Hockin, and to Jon Pearce. The book has been published with the assistance of grants from the Humanities Research Council of Canada, using funds provided by the Canada Council, and from the Publications Fund of University of Toronto Press. Finally I want to thank my husband, Patrick, and my children, Rod, Scott, and Brenda, for their support and good humour.

THE HAUNTED WILDERNESS

Introduction

Anyone aware of the burgeoning interest in Canadian fiction over the past few years is likely aware of a corresponding increase in analysis. Through brief forays and more extensive encounters, a variety of critics have explored the territory, leaving us some sophisticated and scholarly accounts. Yet it is a mistake to assume that our guides, however compelling, are comprehensive. A random perusal of a number of studies will indicate that by and large critics overplay the realistic side of Canadian fiction, frequently associating its achievement with the growth of realism. Books most often discussed, moreover, are those in which the realism has a sociological direction – those which attempt to reflect the social fabric of the land.[1]

The emphasis can partly be explained as a reaction to the seeming artificiality and shallow escapism of much of our early fiction, and a subsequent appreciation of writing firmly rooted in the common clay of everyday experience. Growing feelings of nationalism and the desire for a recognizable cultural identity have further shifted attention towards writing which accurately defines an aspect of our national life.

Whatever the reasons, we have largely neglected an important, unrealistic dimension in Canadian fiction, namely the dark band of gothicism which stretches from earliest to recent times. Some attention has been paid, it is true, to the gothic elements in individual English-Canadian works, and the gothic quality of recent French-Canadian literature is often mentioned, but analysis has been slight. Critics such as Margaret Atwood and D.G. Jones repeatedly head towards the subject only to veer off.[2] Generally, gothicism has been regarded as an idiosyncratic outcropping or, in Quebec novels, as a temporary phenomenon, rather than part of a recurring pattern.

There are a number of problems connected with analyzing this pattern, the first one having to do with terminology. With the passage of time, words often gather a variety of associations so that the original precision of meaning is diffused or lost. Occasionally a literary word begins to be useful as a critical term at the same time as it ceases to be useful as a historical term. Such is the case with 'gothic,' particularly as it applied to the discussion of fiction. Moreover the difficulty surrounding 'gothic' is compounded by its continual association with 'grotesque.'

The original application of both 'gothic' and 'grotesque' was in the areas of art and architecture, an application which continues today. As a literary term, 'gothic' was first used in the early eighteenth century as a supposed characteristic of the Middle Ages and referred to a romantic as opposed to classical style of writing.[3] Originally a term of reprobation, whether with reference to architecture, art, or literature, 'gothic' stood for something barbarous, unpolished, or in bad taste. It began to acquire a more favourable meaning, however, with the publication in 1768 of Horace Walpole's *The Castle of Otranto*, which in the second edition was subtitled *A Gothic Story*. *The Castle of Otranto* began a flood of gothic works which continued until the eighteen-twenties. With Horace Walpole and his imitators, of whom Ann Radcliffe was the foremost craftsman, the term became associated with the tale of gloom and terror. The writing of 'Monk' Lewis and others of the *Schauer-Romantik* (Horror-Romantic) phase shifted its association toward crude or exotic presentations of the macabre, and an extravagant, lurid violence; gothicism represented the 'chambers of horror.'[4] In the writings of this period, the horror was often connected with grotesque features, from the laboratory-manufactured monster in Mary Shelley's *Frankenstein* (1818) to the cannibalistic captives and tortured victims in Maturin's *Melmoth the Wanderer* (1820). It is this element of horrifying grotesqueness which is of particular relevance to modern varieties of gothic writing as, for instance, in the work of Kafka and in the fiction of the American South.

Although the pattern of the gothic story established by Walpole, Radcliffe, and Lewis passed out of favour with the growing popularity of Walter Scott's romances, short tales which had their own gothic elements continued to have appeal, and 'gothic' became associated with these fragments as well. Moreover the influence of the early gothic writers continued through the nineteenth century, so that many late Romantic works have characteristics which are frequently called gothic. Thus as some of the machinery of the gothic novels continued to turn up and to be defined as gothic in the literature of succeeding ages, the term itself became broadened, shifting from a historical to a critical meaning. Increasingly, 'gothic' came to stand for a certain mood of terror or horror, in which the dark mysteries of life were brought to the fore.

John Ruskin's nineteenth-century discussion of gothicism in *The Stones of Venice*[5] was based on his appraisal of certain types of architecture, but it has had considerable influence on the literary use of the term, perhaps because of Ruskin's dual role as art critic and literary critic. For Ruskin, the soul of the gothic mode was characterized by various mental characteristics of the builder, which he placed in order of importance as savageness, changefulness, naturalism, grotesqueness, rigidity, and redundance. According to Ruskin, the withdrawal of any one or two of those qualities would not destroy the gothic character; the removal of a majority of them would.

Although Sigmund Freud, like Ruskin, was formed by the nineteenth century, his influence was really upon the twentieth century. Freud made no direct pronouncements about gothicism, but his teachings and those of his followers have had an indirect impact on the understanding of gothic literature, providing a psychological meaning for it. The actions and machinery of gothic fiction have come to be seen as objective correlatives of a psychic state as, for example, the connection of thunder with an enraged father figure, whether earthly or divine, or Leslie Fiedler's interpretation of the dungeon as 'the womb from whose darkness the ego first emerged.'[6]

Freudian thought has been used by some modern critics to explain the appeal of gothicism. For instance, Davendra Varma admits the possibility that the sentiments expressed in the gothic novel reflect the neurotic and erotic sensibility of the age, claiming that 'the persecution of innocent females, so much a feature of the gothic novels, is at bottom an erotic impulse.'[7] Nevertheless Varma prefers to see the gothic in spiritual terms as a 'quest for the numinous,' an appeal 'to the night side of the soul,' and a 'profound source of the sublime.' Whether or not modern critics associate gothicism with submerged or supernatural levels of experience, they generally emphasize its essentially subjective and symbolic nature in the exploration of the dark side of life.

It is not surprising that there have been connections made between gothic and surrealistic art. The exaggerated contrast of light and dark and of colour and line, as well as the juxtaposition of disparate images, are common to both. Similarly the surrealistic artist's interest in the unconscious world as the real world, and his subsequent exploration of dreams, may be connected to the nightmare quality of gothic literature. Leaders of the surrealist movement, such as André Breton, were clearly admirers of gothic fiction and saw surrealism as a descendant of the early gothic romances. Nevertheless, it can be argued that the anti-supernatural bent of surrealism disallows any close relationship between it and gothicism.

Aside from its spiritual and psychological associations, 'gothic' has also been given a social connotation. Thus gothic writing, particularly that of Europe, has sometimes been seen as a complex, revolutionary form of insight.[8] At other times it has been viewed as reactionary in a broad sense, since it turns back to a romantic vision of the past, particularly the medieval period, with its mystery, mysticism, and supernatural adventures. Yet on the whole, the social connotation of gothicism is played down by critics, and even where it is affirmed (as with Fiedler) the insistence is upon society seen through the distorting mirror of the self, with the exaggerating intensity of personal, psychic, or spiritual urgings.

It is evident, then, that a working definition of the gothic must encompass the variations in its use and be applicable to contemporary gothic writing as well as to the old eighteenth-century English and European models. Despite their differences, there are common elements in what critics through the ages have seen as gothic, and these provide the basis for my usage. 'Gothic' refers here to a subjective view of the dark side of life, seen through the distorting mirror of the self, with its submerged levels of psychic and spiritual experiences. Non-realistic and essentially symbolic in its approach, the gothic opens up various possibilities of psychological, spiritual, or social interpretation. Its mood is pre-eminently one of terror or horror.

As with 'gothic,' the term 'grotesque' was used in connection with the visual arts long before it was applied to literature.[9] Late in the fifteenth century a group of fantastic ornamental paintings and sculptures was discovered in the Grotto of the Baths of Titus. They depicted many monstrous and unnatural forms of pagan animal, vegetable, and human life; creatures half-human and half-animal were common. In sixteenth-century Italy there were many imitations of these grotto paintings and architectural details, and their combination of playful and sinister distortions came to be considered 'grotesque.'

'Grotesque' became accepted as an independent English term during the seventeenth century, but there were many different connotations in use. Even in a literary context it usually retained its connection with art, although gradually the word 'grotesque' served for fantastic and unnatural conceptions in different spheres of thought.[10] In the eighteenth century, 'grotesque' was used in conjunction with growing popular taste for the irrational in literature. For neo-classical critics from Dryden to Shaftesbury, it was a badge of disapproval standing for a perversion of truth; that is, for extravagance, fantasy, and the irrational rejection of the natural order.[11]

Gradually, as Romanticism became a force, the grotesque gained approval as an aspect of the gothic. When Edgar Allan Poe chose to label his 1840 collection of stories *Tales of the Grotesque and Arabesque*, he indicated in the preface that 'grotesque' and 'arabesque' were used synonymously to indicate the gloomy tenor and Germanism of the tales. Along with this general approval of the grotesque in the nineteenth century, there came an accretion of new meanings. The most important uses of the term were those of Coleridge and Ruskin. The latter especially has had a lasting influence on the general understanding of the grotesque among both nineteenth-century and twentieth-century critics.

Coleridge used 'grotesque' in connection with medieval gothicism, but his main contribution was his specific definition of it as a comic term.[12] Ruskin produced a highly systematic and complicated approach to the grotesque, which he saw as a purely aesthetic term rather than an attribute of nature.[13] Like Coleridge, he viewed the grotesque as a comic genre, but he insisted on an element of fearfulness juxtaposed with ludicrousness. The two species of grotesque, the terrible and the sportive, depended on the predominant element of fearfulness or ludicrousness. Underlying Ruskin's discussion of the grotesque is the idea that all forms of what he called 'noble' or true grotesque have a spiritual quality. Unlike the ignoble grotesque, which is sensual, frivolous, and rooted in vice, the noble grotesque arises from man's necessarily limited and thus distorted intuition of supernatural truth.

In the twentieth century, the grotesque has become an ever more frequent mode among writers. At the same time the definition of grotesqueness, like that of gothicism, now includes new psychological and philosophical ideas. Increasingly it has been linked to cosmic pointlessness of the kind exhibited in the dramas of Pirandello and his followers in the Theatre of the Absurd. Thus Wolfgang Kayser provides a three-fold definition of the grotesque as the estranged world, a play with the absurd, and an attempt to invoke and subdue the demonic aspects in the world.[14] By contrast with this absurdist perspective, Flannery O'Connor proposes that the writer with Christian faith will be most inclined toward the grotesque, as a result of his awareness of the distortion of modern life.[15] Moreover, although Kayser attempts a distinction between the grotesque and the tragic by suggesting the meaninglessness behind the former and the possibility of meaning in the latter, other critics suggest that the grotesque is simply a merging of the comic and the tragic.[16]

Obviously there is no clear agreement about the meaning given the term 'grotesque.' It has been connected to a quality of writing, to a type of writer, to a particular world view, and to actual conditions of life. Yet despite some arbitrariness in selection, it is possible to provide a working definition of the grotesque as an aesthetic term, referring to a mode of writing rather than a condition or attribute of nature: the grotesque emphasizes incongruity, disorder, and deformity, and arises from the juxtaposition or clash of the ideal with the real, the psychic with the physical, or the concrete with the symbolic. Whether there is an underlying order in the writer's grotesque view of life or whether he writes from a position of meaninglessness, he presents a distorted picture of the world. Sometimes given a transcendent reference, the grotesque can be seen as an indirect search for a higher reality or the sublime via the unconscious or demonic region of the mind. Although it has been associated at times with comic exaggeration which is pure fun, the usual interpretation, and the one I shall follow, insists upon a horrifying or fearful aspect, linking it with the gothic.

Even this brief a synopsis of the history of 'gothic' and 'grotesque' shows the reason for the frequent overlap or confusion in their usage.[17] Both terms involve a subjective and often symbolic vision of experience which invokes feelings of fear or horror, although the grotesque may frequently have a comic side as well. Both suggest distortions in characterization, although the grotesque leans to visual ugliness and bizarre juxtapositions, whereas the gothic may only give two-dimensional portraits with emphasis on a few exaggerated qualities. Both the gothic and the grotesque present mysterious, non-rational levels of experience, whether one chooses to call these the dark side of the soul, the night side of life, or the impulses of the id; both react against the conventional ordering of reality, seeking in strange ways a truth beyond the accepted surface of life. Sin and death are the dominant themes of both. Yet, although the gothic and the grotesque are closely related, I consider the gothic to be the more inclusive category or genre, embracing all works in which terror or horror are major elements. The grotesque thus becomes a mode of the gothic, although with its growing importance in twentieth-century literature it begins to be a genre in its own right.

This study of the gothic and grotesque in Canadian fiction provides a critical analysis rather than a historical survey. The number of works given detailed treatment is limited, and the focus is upon varieties of gothic fiction rather than upon authors inclined towards gothicism. Although the criteria for selection was not primarily literary merit, I have attempted to choose books which have a permanent place in Canadian fiction. Obviously it is more difficult to assess the long-term significance of the large number of contemporary books with gothic-grotesque features than to choose the earlier nineteenth-century books, since those which have survived thus far are not likely to fade from view altogether.

Where possible, English translations of French works are used, and popular editions are the basis of all the analyses. *Wacousta* and *The Golden Dog* are the only works where the latter policy makes a difference, since the popular edition is in each case an abridgement of the original edition. Unfortunately, unabridged editions of these two books are not readily available. Although the original texts have been consulted, and brief critiques of the differences in the editions are given in the notes, it seemed wise to keep to the aim of discussing books which are in general circulation.

Obviously many romances and novels are not gothic in any way, and there is no intention of providing a prescriptive lens through which all Canadian fiction can be viewed. The various categories have not been taken from any prior categorization of gothic fiction and imposed upon the material. Rather they arose from a careful examination of the works themselves. Although some of the headings correspond to those used by other writers – as, for example, the divisions of the grotesque used by Ruskin – the overall arrangement is unique to this study. Moreover my attempt is to explore and speculate upon the material available rather than to batten it all down in a tightly ordered scheme. From the examination of key books presenting different facets of the subject, general comments as well as new questions emerge. The conclusion is not intended to bring us back full circle, but to provide a reflective pause in a critical probe which has progressed some distance from its initial point of departure, while at the same time suggesting further areas of worthwhile investigation.

PART ONE

NINETEENTH-CENTURY GOTHIC FICTION

1
Early Gothic

For many readers in the last century, the appeal of fiction was the appeal of the romance. In an era when an emotional response to life was considered an attribute if not a prerequisite of virtue, it is not surprising that there was a demand for stories with suspense and sensation, which would afford the thrill of strong emotional engagement. The romance supplied fast-paced plots and melodramatic characters who were larger than life in their villainy or virtue.

Because of its emphasis on the improbable or fantastic, most critics see the romance as a contrasting stream of fiction from the novel. Wellek and Warren are typical in their comments:

The two types, which are polar, indicate the double descent of prose narrative: the novel develops from the lineage of non-fictitious narrative forms – the letter, the journal, the memoir or biography, the chronicle or history; it develops, so to speak, out of documents; stylistically, it stresses representative detail, mimesis in its narrow sense. The romance, on the other hand, the continuator of the epic and the medieval romance, may neglect verisimilitude of detail ... addressing itself to a higher reality, a deeper psychology.[1]

Although such categories are helpful in distinguishing varieties of fiction, clearly there are significant deviations within each form. Thus the nineteenth-century novel of manners and morals may have an overlay of melodramatic incident and sentimentality which might properly be termed 'romantic'; similarly the romance includes wide variations.

Although all romance strikes an emotional chord, it makes a difference whether the chord is in a minor or a major key. Compared to the gothic romance, with its frightening mood of mystery or estrangement, the sentimental romance has an atmosphere of optimism rather than doom, with a final reassurance of conventional sentiments and attitudes. As Leslie Fiedler has illustrated,[2] where the gothic romance raises the spectre of inscrutable evil, often exemplified by incest and other unnatural relationships, the sentimental romance presents the ideal of chaste love and virtue triumphant. If the former resembles a nightmare, the latter seems an idealistic dream. Yet since both types spring basically from the same imaginative fount, it is not surprising that gothic elements are repeatedly found in the sentimental romance and vice versa.

The confusion of the gothic with the sentimental is readily observable in the numerous early Canadian romances. Moreover, as nineteenth-century writers increasingly became interested in historical romances, the fictional spectrum broadened further. Although romances generally used the past as, in Hawthorne's words, 'a poetic precinct where actualities would not be insisted upon,'[3] many historical romances emphasized historical details for their own sake, treating the externals as real objects and occurrences. In this respect they moved closer to the novel.

A contrast can be made between English-Canadian and French-Canadian uses of history, although as is ever the case with general statements, there are striking exceptions on both sides. Although the historical romances of both cultures moved into gothic realms, English Canadians tended to use the past as a vivid backdrop for exciting adventure and to be interested in the details of early French Canada as fascinating, factual curios. The French Canadians, by comparison, idealized the past and exploited it for didactic purposes. For French-Canadian novelists as well as historians, history has been and is looked upon 'as a tool for shaping the present,'[4] and thus history has always played a very special role in their fiction.

François-Xavier Garneau's *Histoire du Canada*,[5] the first volume of which appeared in 1845, was the primary influence upon the first flowering of French-Canadian literature. Garneau's romanticizing of a glorious past, with its grand adventures and its heroes and heroines, was essentially, as Ramsay Cook points out,[6] a conservative prescription for survival, a rallying cry for traditional religion, laws, and nationality. Good men and bad are clearly drawn according to this prescription, a simplified dramatization which was to be picked up and carried forward by the writers of romance.

For English-Canadian romances, the didactic purpose was not as dominant, William Kirby's work being a partial exception. Kenneth Windsor indicates that there was often an underlying liberal bias in such novels,[7] fed by the historical writing of Goldwin Smith and particularly of Frances Parkman, whose epic, *France and England in North America*,[8] became the primary interpretation for English-Canadians of the old régime in Quebec. In Parkman's eyes, 'a happier calamity never befell a people' than the French Canadians' conquest by the English, a struggle which pitted Anglo-Saxon liberty, progress, and intellectual vitality against Roman Catholic absolutism and moral and intellectual torpor. This sense of the inevitable victory of the modern concepts of progress and liberty unconsciously underlay the thinking of many fictional treatments of Quebec, as, for example, in the work of Gilbert Parker. Nevertheless English-Canadian writers on the whole were more interested in history for its colour and excitement than for its ideological potential.

Important to any discussion of early Canadian gothicism, or of romance in general, is the place of folk tales and legends, especially those of Quebec. Folk tales dominated the literature and para-literature of nineteenth-century French-Canadian writing, but they were also very evident in many English-Canadian romances with French-Canadian settings. Ostensibly the legends and tales appealed to writers as reminders of a colourful past. Yet in his examination of Quebec tales, Jean Rigeault states that the folk tales' insistence on a religious moral is one of their predominant features.[9] A glance at any of the various collections reveals the frequency of religious injunctions. Moreover the frequent didacticism in the introduction and conclusion acts as moral book ends, attempting to squeeze the tale into a spiritually ordered framework in which conventional Catholic beliefs and practices are brought to the fore.[10]

In introducing his collection of tales and legends, *Forestiers et voyageurs*, J.-C. Taché insists that the French-Canadian values imparted by the tales and legends are a basic part of the voyageurs' education.[11] At the same time he acknowledges that the term 'voyageur' does not simply mean a man who has travelled far or frequently; it also means 'un homme du tempérament aventureux.' Jack Warwick takes the latter statement even further,[12] associating the voyageur with the recurring literary concept of 'pays d'en haut' – a symbolic as much as geographic area which stands for expansive vigour and possibilities without bound, as well as for moral confusion or rebellion. If, therefore, the voyageur popularly represented a kind of moral as well as social venturesomeness, it seems strange that the tales which issued from his milieu have such an insistent moralistic aspect. Remembering that the tales were orally transmitted rather than written, one wonders if those people responsible for collecting and writing down the tales were also responsible for the moralizing additives.

This suspicion becomes stronger with the realization that the primary impression left by the tales is not so much that of spiritual security – of faith triumphant or virtue rewarded – but of the overwhelming power of evil. A gothic mood of terror or horror frequently dominates. Evil, often personified in strange disguises, at times plays such an aggressive role that the tales seem Manichaean. The collections of folk tales suggest that the collectors themselves recognized this voyageur spirit of rebellious freedom – the encounter with unaccountable evil or mystery and its resultant sense of moral confusion or uncertainty – as the lifeblood of the tales. They may have attempted, therefore, to contain or subdue this spirit with a heavy dose of traditional piety and religious teaching. Despite the moral encasement, the energy of the tale issues from its story of the adventures of characters living beyond the confines of conventional social and religious securities; the dangerous libertine spirit bursts through, with its fascination as a vital force and its terror as a mysterious, disruptive power.

As a means of understanding the diversity of gothicism in nineteenth-century Canadian fiction, I have singled out for special analysis John Richardson's *Wacousta*, William Kirby's *The Golden Dog*, Philippe Aubert de Gaspé's *Le Chercheur de trésors*, and J.P. Tardivel's *For My Country: Pour la patrie*. Each represents a different aspect of the gothic tradition in Canada. Of course many other works have gothic features. On the French-Canadian side, the stream of sentimental, patriotic romances, which at times threatened to become a flood, was rarely without an incident or character most properly described as gothic in manner if not in spirit. For instance, *Les Anciens Canadiens* by Aubert de Gaspé (père)[13] provides us with the tale of La Corriveau and a belief in witches sufficiently serious to warrant Jules's remark to the young Lochiel: 'The difference is, my dear boy, that in Scotland you burn them, while here we treat them in a manner fitting their power and social influence.' One of the most exciting moments in this story, when Dumas is caught in the raging, icy current, presents a tableau of the essential conflict between conventional spiritual safeguards and the forces of destruction evident in so many French-Canadian works. To Jules, the central hero, 'this human being suspended on the verge of the bellowing gulf, this venerable priest administering from afar under the open heaven the sacrament of penance, the anguished prayers, the sublime invocation; all seem to him a dreadful dream.' In its symbolic implications, one can feel an element of gothic terror creeping into the sentimental story.

Even as sentimental a romance as Marmette's *François de Bienville*,[14] published in 1870, contains the ferocious Indian, Dent-de-Loup, whose evil motives and methods reveal him as a satanic antichrist. Marmette's writing shows the dramatic impact of Fenimore Cooper, especially in its employment of the forest as a place of mystery, terror, and sudden shock, a gothic motif also found in Doutre's *Les Fiancés de 1812*,[15] first published in 1844. Pamphile Lemay's novel in verse, *Les Vengeances*[16] (1875), has perhaps the most obvious and repeated use of gothic motifs of all French-Canadian fiction in the last century, and in many ways, from its central theme of vengeance to its contrast of natural and civilized life, recalls Richardson's *Wacousta*.

Among English-Canadian writers who made literary excursions into gothic territory, Gilbert Parker deserves particular mention. As with Kirby, Parker's best-known works are set in French Canada; *The Seats of the Mighty* (1896),[17] like

The Golden Dog, uses traditional gothic motifs in exploring the evils which beset the 'ancien régime.' Of interest as a comparison to *Le Chercheur de trésors* is Parker's *When Valmond Came to Pontiac* (1895),[18] which not only uses folk material as does *Le Chercheur de trésors*, but also combines in its basically rustic hero the tragicomic mixture and the single-minded distorting vision common in the grotesque figures of modern literature, as, for example, in William Faulkner's fiction.

Although the particular examination of four books does not pretend to reveal the full range of gothicism, these representative and relatively well-known works illustrate that the gothic mode, despite the passing of its eighteenth-century, European heyday, held more than a residual appeal for Canadian as well as European and American writers. They provide basic evidence that beside the attachment to sentimental fiction in the nineteenth century and the growth of realism, the urge for darker fantasy, in which the terrible and terrifying promptings of the spirit could be imaginatively recreated, was a continuing, countervailing literary force.

2

Canadian Prototype: *Wacousta*

From John Richardson's military training and his familiarity with actual details of incident and geography, one might expect a realistic account of events in his writings. His first major work, *The War of 1812*,[1] is indeed a non-fictional narrative with a realistic and vivid portrayal of military operations. *Wacousta; or, The Prophecy*,[2] first published in 1832, is also based on an actual historical event, Pontiac's attempt to seize those last two British forts, Detroit and Michilimackinac. Despite the conventional authorial disclaimer that 'all else is imaginary,' Richardson is at pains in his introduction to the 1851 edition to justify the inclusion of two unrealistic details – the 'improbability' of Wacousta's feat with the flagstaff, and the 'geographical error' of the narrowed St Clair River.[3]

Nevertheless *Wacousta* is assuredly more of a gothic romance than a realistic novel. It might be argued that the actualities of life in America at the time of Pontiac have a melodramatic quality exceeding the fantasies of romance, that the historical truth is stranger than gothic fiction. Klinck talks of 'this surfeit of the spectacular, this incredible profusion of New World "Gothic" material,' and of the 'storybook lustre' which historical documentation acquires when relating the facts of actual people and incidents in the early days of North American settlement.[4] Following this line of thinking, one might maintain that in fictionalizing events of the sort Richardson chose, attempted verisimilitude will inevitably appear romantic.

Critics have suggested that the gothicism in *Wacousta* can be traced to the 'outrages of mind and heart experienced by Richardson when he was a boy at war in the forests of the Canadian border.'[5] Although any discussion which attempts to understand an author's work by relating it to his life is a risky business, when one considers that Richardson was only fifteen when thrust into the middle of savage and strange warfare,[6] it is not unlikely that a feeling of overwhelming terror should have left its mark on him and on his writings.

Yet *Wacousta*'s gothic romanticism is not so much related to its melodramatic externals, whether historically or autobiographically based, as to the affecting symbolic power of these externals; the central images in the tale are correlatives of a terror of the spirit which is gothic in its proportions. This is not to deny the gothic surface of Richardson's romance; on the level of motifs, *Wacousta* assuredly fits into the traditional pattern. The epigraph which appeared in the first edition is obviously gothic in its mention of Vengeance, who 'stalks' from her 'dark covert' with snakes, familiar symbol of evil, upon her chest. Wacousta himself is the outcast obsessed with revenge and an example of the conventional formula, apparent in characterizations from Faust to Frankenstein, of the heroic villain beset with a demonic compulsion. The numerous scenes of flight and chase, from the early unsuccessful pursuit of the garrison's night intruder, to Madeline's escape from the beseiged Fort Michilimackinac, to Wacousta's continued pursuit of the de Haldimar family, recall similar scenes in the tales of Walpole, Lewis, or Poe. A common gothic feature is the ghostly apparition, found here in the ghoulish face, suddenly appearing to the 'horror and dismay' of the sailor:

Through an opening in the foliage peered the pale and spectral face of a human being with its dull eyes bent fixedly and mechanically upon the vessel ... The pallid mouth was partially unclosed, so as to display a row of white and apparently lipless teeth, and the features were otherwise set and drawn, as those of one who is no longer of earth. (p 197)

Typically gothic also are the gory scenes of slaughter, as with the grotesque description of the fight aboard the schooner: 'A heavy blow from his cutlass accompanied these words, the fingers divided at their very roots, rolled to the bottom of the boat and the carcass of the savage dropped with a yell of anguish far in the rear.' Violent encounters and sudden deaths are, of course, standard events in the gothic repertoire.

Amid this pattern of gothic motifs, however, Richardson sometimes seems to retreat from his revelations of demonic darkness. As if to counterbalance those scenes in which real depths of gothic terror burst to the surface, he introduces scenes in which romantic cliché and sentimental feeling seem designed to create a more bland atmosphere. It is possible that the sentimentalism here reflects the popular appetite for sentimental romances which followed in the wake of Sir Walter Scott's enormous success. Whether or not Richardson was bowing to the prevailing taste remains speculation, but, in any event, the combination of sentimental and gothic motifs in *Wacousta* is common in nineteenth-century Canadian fiction, as it is elsewhere.

The gothic spirit repeatedly bursts back through the sentimental scenes, as is evident in the passages describing the relationships between members of the garrison community. Here the theme of sentimental love is emphasized, with that unsullied goddess, the 'gentle Clara,' fulfilling the role of sexless purity. The typical evasion of physical love in the historical romance is especially evident in the relationship between Clara and Valletort; and in the described reunion of the two in the forest Richardson himself seems compelled to give an explanation. He offers the conventional apology that 'there are emotions of the heart it would be mocking in the pen to trace.' Nevertheless, as in many historical romances where passion's only respectable showing is at death, in *Wacousta* there is a loosening of the corsets of propriety in the final meeting between Clara and Valletort, when death for both is around the corner.

Although the lack of sexual encounter between lovers is replaced by a sentimental tie between brother and sister – Charles and Clara de Haldimar – and between the two cousins, Clara and Madeline, the relationships have gothic undercurrents. Between Charles and Clara, there is a subtle suggestion of incest, a perverse relationship which, as Fiedler has demonstrated, is at the heart of many a gothic tale, and which he describes as a deliberate 'challenge to the most sacred of bourgeois taboos.'[7] In chapter 6 particularly, when Charles reveals his affection for his beloved sister, the romantic sentiment has incestuous undercurrents.[8] We are informed that whenever he extolled the virtues and accomplishments of Clara, 'then indeed would his usually calm, blue eyes sparkle with the animation of his subject, while his colouring cheek marked all the warmth and sincerity with which he bore attestation to her gentleness and her goodness.' Later, declaring his happiness in Valletort's successful suit of his sister, he says, 'My sister Clara I adore with all the affection of my nature! I love her better than my own life, which is wrapped up in hers.'

Considering the femininity of Charles's appearance at the time of his pronounced pleasure in the match, one suspects also that this happiness at a prospective union of his 'dearer half' with his best friend contains homosexual implications:

Never had Charles appeared so eminently handsome; and yet his beauty resembled that of a frail and delicate woman rather than one called to the manly and arduous profession of a soldier. The large, blue, long dark-lashed eye in which a share of languor harmonized with the soft but animated expression of the whole countenance – the dimpled mouth – the small, clear, and even teeth – all these now characterized Charles de Haldimar; and if to these we add a voice rich, full and melodious, and a smile sweet and fascinating, we shall be at no loss to account for the readiness with which Sir Everard suffered his imagination to draw on the brother for those attributes he ascribed to the sister. (p 66)

Similarly, despite the happy reunion and marriage between Frederick and Madeline at the end of the story, and the sentimental vision of wedded bliss, there is a peculiar lesbian twist to the sexual cliché used in describing the reunion of Madeline and Clara: 'The former threw herself impetuously on the bosom of the sobbing girl Clara, who, with extended arms, parted lips and heaving bosom, sat breathlessly awaiting the first dawn of the returning reason of her more than sister.'

The unmistakably gothic dimension of *Wacousta*, and Richardson's belated attempt to contain it, are also evident in the depiction of the central character. From his initial appearance, Wacousta is described as an almost superhuman figure of satanic defiance, whose huge presence commands awesome respect as well as increasing terror. In his challenge to the little enclave of civilization, he represents the mysterious, menacing power of evil and death, as is evident in the description of his arrival at the garrison: 'His face was painted black as death, and as he stood under the arch of the gateway, with his white turbaned head towering far above those of his companions, this formidable mysterious enemy might have been likened to the spirit of darkness presiding over his terrible legions.'

As befits many a gothic villain from 'Monk' Lewis's Ambrosio onward,[9] Wacousta has a highly developed sexuality. During the forest scene, in which he decides to make Clara his wife 'without the solemnization of these tedious forms,' the sexual atmosphere is startling considering the age and society in which the book was written. Wacousta's unbridled sexuality is evidently designed to reinforce the impression of his savagery, just as the description of Ellen passionately throwing herself upon the prostrate Wacousta heightens the horror of her derangement.

Yet it is clear that Wacousta's sexuality is not by itself the source of gothic terror, but is associated with his overpowering will. It is rape Clara refers to when she says she 'fears something more than death' at the hands of the savages. In Canadian gothic fiction, as will be seen throughout this study, despite the strong Calvinistic emphasis on bodily depravity, the deepest form of terror emanates from a demonic wilfulness. Although this wilfulness is often manifested as sexual aggression, it is the will more than the sex which seems satanic.

Nevertheless, despite the decorous shudderings and bitter sighings of the fainting captive Clara, the forest scene builds toward a sexual as well as dramatic climax. Suddenly this advance is halted by the long-winded revelation of Wacousta's identity, and subsequently by the intervention of the rescuing soldiers. The dénouement, in which Wacousta is discovered to be Sir Reginald Morton, is an abrupt switch to sentimentality. It has all the sentimental attributes of a Scott tale, even to the romantic scenery of the Scottish Highlands. Morton is the genteel primitive who feels 'a wild and fearful triumph' in the deer hunt – a respectable sport, nonetheless. His dear love, Clara Beverley, true to romantic decorum combines wildness with 'elegance' and 'classic' harmony, and is discovered on a bank 'covered with moss and interspersed with wild roses and honeysuckle.'

At this revelation of his true past, Wacousta shrivels from his gothic role to appear as an ordinary, wronged man, conscious of respectability and intent on returning to the community. Significantly, his face shows the change from the gothic to the sentimental, for 'there was now a shade of melancholy mixed with the fierceness of expression usually observable there.' No longer the demonic, Faustian figure, he becomes a sorrowing ex-soldier, anxious to die with his boots back on. The death of Wacousta when, defiant once again, he falls from the bridge, is perhaps a belated attempt by Richardson to recover lost gothic ground. Shown etched in relief against the background, Wacousta's 'gigantic proportions' and vengeful war cry restore his image as a terrifying force, although his death fits the sentimental requirement that the villain get his just deserts.

The ending seems a failure of nerve on Richardson's part rather than a fitting conclusion to the tale. It is a forced resolution, removed from the spirit of the earlier part of the book. The emotional centre of the book is in its gothic revelation of wilful evil, mystery, sexuality, and darkness; the dominant mood is one of terror rather than sentimental love.

One indication of Richardson's real interest in the gothic mid-section is the better quality of its writing. The scenes of violence and suspense are clearly less artificial or laden with cliché in dialogue and description than the love scenes; the writing is generally crisper and the dramatic effects skilfully and originally handled. Carl Klinck notes the rhythm of suspense and surprise which is a distinctive feature of the book and a key to its deepest impression: 'Eyes and ears are constantly strained for movement and sound. The silences, notably in the forest, are nerve-wracking, and they are shattered with melodramatic abruptness.'[10] An example of this abrupt shock technique occurs in chapter 19, when there is a repeated alteration of hushed expectant silence and the sudden war cries of the Indians, a suspenseful crisis when 'the silence that now prevailed was strongly in contrast with and even more fearful than the horrid shouts of which it had been preceded.' Richardson has obviously learned the lesson of Mrs Radcliffe, who first so effectively alternated sound and silence and light and dark as a means of creating her gothic atmosphere. The influence of Fenimore Cooper or his many imitators is also evident in this use of sudden surprise.

The attitude to nature in *Wacousta* is particularly revealing of its gothic mood. Although nature is an enveloping presence in the book, there is little detailed description of its particulars. Rather it has an abstract, symbolic quality. At the same time, Richardson exhibits towards nature an ambiguity which is the mark of true gothicism. His attitude combines fascination with horror, seeing nature as a source of exciting vigour and also of ominous danger or doom. It is an attitude which recurs in numerous later books to the present day, and may well be identified as typically Canadian. Frye has remarked on the 'deep tone of terror' in Canadian poetry in regard to nature: 'It is not a terror of the danger or discomforts or even of the mysteries of nature, but a terror of the soul at something that these things manifest.'[11] While this may be a perceptive commentary on much Canadian poetry, in fiction, at least, the response to nature is usually more complex.

It is true that in *Wacousta* a profound fear of nature often seems to override any other response, and nature seems to symbolize all the inscrutable, evil forces of life. The dark covert of the epigraph, from which evil vengeance springs, is the forest wilderness. It in turn is haunted by the Indians, the irrational children of nature, who at times appear as gothic embodiments of inscrutable demonism; they are referred to variously as 'devilish savages,' 'images of death in their most appalling shapes,' and 'whooping hell-fiends.' Yet at other times the energy and splendour of nature and her people are attractive. For example, there is an admiring description of the blockhouse apartment, so unlike any 'modern European boudoir' with its ingenious specimens of Indian art, its 'headdresses tastefully wrought in the shape of the crowing bays of the ancients and composed of the gorgeous feathers of the most splendid of the forest birds.' One notices also the double response to the appearance of the Indians on Lake Huron, a scene particularly reminiscent of Fenimore Cooper's fiction:

the light swift bark canoes of the natives often danced joyously on its surface, and while the sight was offended at the savage skulking among the trees of the forest, like some dark spirit moving cautiously in its course of secret destruction, and watching the moment when he might pounce unnoticed upon his unprepared victim, it followed with momentary pleasure and excitement the activity and skill displayed by the harmless paddler in the swift and meteor-like race that set the troubled Huron in a sheet of hissing foam. (p 159)

Ellen Holloway and Wacousta himself symbolically indicate the ambivalence of Richardson's response to nature. In one way they suggest the destructiveness of natural life. Both are people with natural passion who attempt a marriage based on heart rather than head. Both end their days among the primitives of nature, the Indians. The picture given of the 'natural life' in the forest is far from the romantic notion of the 'noble savage,' and Richardson makes an apparent equation here of primitive nature, irrationality, and savagery. Nowhere is Wacousta seen as vicious and rude, and Ellen has sunk to a state of 'negligence and slovenliness.' Her madness is a sign of ultimate estrangement from the world, persistent in gothic literature; her movements are 'altogether mechanical,' and performed 'with almost utter unconsciousness of their action,' a condition of human mechanism to be described again and again in modern grotesque fiction.

But nature is not unequivocally evil. Ellen's unfortunate condition may be viewed as the disastrous result of the suppression of nature, or of man's rationalistic attempt to master it. Wacousta and Ellen have been victimized by the intellectual wilfulness and unnatural heartlessness of Colonel de Haldimar. There is a suggestion that 'civilized' rationality is as much to be feared as primitive nature. Indeed Wacousta is often depicted as a magnificent figure, a 'noble looking warrior' and a 'fine fellow,' who even in his most terrifying conduct has an energetic and awesome presence. One finds a more loathsome, despicable evil in the colonel, the embodiment of the civilized class, who rules with haughty coolness and strict rationalistic observance of rules. Interestingly, Ellen's prophetic voice is directed initially not against the savages in the forests, but against the 'hard-hearted man,' Colonel de Haldimar, and finally against the whole of his 'accursed race.'

Wacousta's gothic terror is therefore not associated simply with nature, but with a feeling of menace from within civilized society as well as from without. The prevailing feeling of menace is revealed in a series of images with which Richardson describes life as 'gloomy and unpenetrable,' and yet the garrison which attempts to shut out the forest accentuates the 'prison-house' atmosphere. This tension between the isolated, dangerous freedom of primitive nature and the sense of claustrophobia of a 'garrison culture' (to use Frye's term) is of course a recurring theme in Canadian literature from Susanna Moodie to contemporary writers.

In the same passage there is also a feeling of nostalgia for past European civilization. Yet ironically, this gloriously remembered 'happiness and liberty' on the other side of the water, whether it be in the garrison or England, cannot be reached. Thus co-existing with the fearful inadequacies of the soldiers' present environment is the haunting fear that 'you can't go home again' to any past model of security.

In the final section of his novel, Richardson presents an image of happy reconciliation between nature and society. Madeline gives a ring to the 'faithful creature' Oucanasta, embracing her with 'deep manifestations of affection,' and the latter in turn is 'sensibly gratified.' Yet this reconciliation is really only an instance of the primitive becoming 'civilized,' and juxtaposed with the rest of the book, it seems forced and laughably sentimental.

It is symbolically and dramatically fitting that the bridge is the scene of much of the important action in *Wacousta*, from the initial execution of Frank Halloway and his wife's prophesying, to the encounter and capture of Wacousta, to the final ghastly fight between the Indian warriors and the soldiers. A narrow passage over the river ravine, with the forest on one side and the town on the other, it is the meeting place of the conflict between two ways of life. Significantly, it is by falling into the abyss below the bridge that Wacousta as well as Clara meet their death; contributing to the gothic horror in *Wacousta* as in other gothic tales is this sense of a precarious footing, insecure and menaced, with a continuing danger of a fall into the abyss of spiritual or cultural doom.

It is a horror which may well be related to Richardson's life, to the cultural shock of frontier living, where European ways seemed patently unsuitable and inadequate, and yet native primitivism presented a terrifying alternative. Like Susanna Moodie, Richardson in *Wacousta* seems to fear a breakdown of the social order, but is without an ideal to seek in either group. This aspect of Richardson's gothicism contrasts with prevalent American and British attitudes, especially of the nineteenth century, and is a repeated characteristic in Canadian gothic fiction, as this study will reveal. In American fiction where there is conflict between the primitive and the civilized, the author most often takes the primitive option – a position seen in Cooper, Thoreau, Melville, Twain, and Faulkner, to name but a few. In English fiction, the necessity of such an option hardly seems to exist, not even in, say, the Brontës, since the social order is nearly always presupposed, whatever the degree of romantic attachment to natural life.

The sense of gothic disorientation or estrangement in a sinister world where there is no protective order has spiritual as well as cultural implications. The fear of spiritual emptiness is vividly illustrated in the passage following the guardhouse slaughter. Although it is a scene which 'might have called up a not inapt image of hell to the bewildered and confounded brain,' yet 'the sun shone in yellow lustre, and all nature smiled and wore an air of calm, as if the accursed deed had had the sanction of heaven and the spirits of light loved to look down upon the frightful atrocities there in perpetration.'

Thus while many of the traditional features of the eighteenth-century gothic tale are retained in *Wacousta*, some of the conventional motifs and symbols have been adapted; the sources and implications of terror reflect Richardson's Canadian experience. *Wacousta* is a worthwhile starting place for this study as a prototype of naturalized, gothic fiction in Canada. Moreover, in the conflict between the gothic and the sentimental it illustrates a common feature of nineteenth-century romances which lingers even today.

The appeal of Richardson's book is in his bold invocation of the lurking terrors of life, his dramatic presentation of its inscrutable forces of evil and doom. Paradoxically, *Wacousta* may be described as an attempt to exorcise these demonic elements.[12] Richardson's attempt fails in the ending of the book, when he covers his fear with a sentimental icing; he may partially succeed in the gothic centre of the book, when the dark forces are challenged by his artistic strength. Richardson's power in *Wacousta* is similar to that which he ascribes to Clara: 'Death, certain death, to all she saw was inevitable, and while her perception at once embraced the futility of all attempts at escape from the general doom, she snatched from despair the power to follow its gloomy details without being annihilated under their weight.'

3

Decorative Gothic: *The Golden Dog*

William Kirby's *The Golden Dog*[1] was published in 1877, a time when interest in
local colour sketches was beginning to rival the popularity of historical romances.
Kirby's book seems an attempt to appeal to both facets of public taste, as well as
to kindle the fires of Canadian patriotism already smouldering in these first years
after Confederation. The result is a form of decorative gothicism.

Like many ardent Tories before and since, Kirby found much to admire in the
old values of Quebec:

in its chivalric conventions, its class distinctions, its loyalty to Crown and Empire,
its traditionalism and in its religious devotion, it embodied a way of life which
Kirby sought vainly to perpetuate.[2]

Through this sympathy with French-Canadian ideals as well as his scholarly interest in French-Canadian life, Kirby was able to escape the condescension which
was apt to cloud the perception of English Canadians fed only on the Whiggish
biases of Parkman's histories.

In *The Golden Dog*, Kirby has obviously done some careful research into life
in Quebec in the days when it was still a colony of France. Many realistic details
of the physical and social environment of the time are interspersed throughout
the book (and especially in the early chapters), from the descriptions of the swin-
dle of the *Friponne* compared with the honest mercantile system of the Bourgeois
Philibert, to the workings of ferry and canoe transportation, to the picture of
cloistered life in the convent of the Ursulines.

There is a particular feeling of verisimilitude in the sharply drawn presentation
of the background characters, as, for example, the regulars in the Taverne de
Menut – Max Grimeau, blind Bartemy, and Master Pothier – whose portraits
Kirby himself likens to those by 'the vulgar but faithful Dutch pencils of Schalken

and Teniers'. One notices especially the sketch of Dame Rochelle, the Bourgeois' worthy housekeeper and strict old Puritan, about whom 'not an end of ribbon or edge of lace could be seen to point to one hair-breadth of indulgence in the vanities of the world'. She might have sprung from a page of Dickens. The influence of Scott and Shakespeare, in their appreciation of the comic possibilities of peasant types, may also lie behind Kirby's skill at character-drawing in his secondary figures. In an attempt to capture the flavour of the time, Kirby has included various elements of French-Canadian folklore, from the legend of la Corriveau to the gay song of the voyageurs who 'made the shores ring' with their chorus of 'V'la l'bon vent!'

Despite these realistic details, *The Golden Dog* has more obviously fantastic, gothic motifs of the European variety than *Wacousta*. Here is the conventional crumbling castle, in this case the chateau of Beaumanoir, that sinister centre of intrigue. The gothic villain, in European and English fiction often a member of the aristocracy, has in this tale both a male and a female version. Both Intendant Bigot and Angélique are seductive types whose hold over others amounts almost to a spell. Le Guardeur, like so many gothic characters, seems obsessed or compulsive in his response to temptations; he appears to be in the grip of some demonic force.

As one often finds in a gothic tale, there is in *The Golden Dog* the witch, La Corriveau, with 'claws like a Harpy,' whose evil is associated with her 'sharp intellect' and craft. Like Frankenstein, she knows too much, and like Bigot and Angélique carried to a chilling extreme, she is ever calculating, with an unnatural, hard heart. Thus as with Colonel de Haldimar in *Wacousta*, or Hawthorne's Chillingworth, it is not an excess of passion as much as an overbalance of head over heart which leads to evil; the urge to control drives humans beyond the limits of humanity.

Similarly, the will to power drives Angélique into a pact with the devil. The descriptions of Angélique and Amélie show a deliberate parallelism, suggesting symbolic meaning in their characterizations and setting in relief those features which are dissimilar. They are both tall and graceful, fashioned in 'perfect symmetry' and with an ease of movement. However, one is light in colouring and the other dark; one is suggestive of 'spiritual graces' and the other of 'terrestrial witchiness.'

An aura of gothicism is also present in the chapter headings, as blatantly melodramatic as to be comic; for example, 'Silk Gloves on Bloody Hands,' and the Poe-inspired 'Quoth the Raven Nevermore.' The episodes themselves are no less melodramatic. Chapter 34 especially, in which Caroline is murdered, brings together an array of familiar motifs. The episode reveals a treacherous poisoning by the disguised witch, La Corriveau, who comes by stealth to the gloomy chateau with its grated windows and gains entrance to the hidden vault. There she murders by deadly flowers the white-clothed maiden.

Finally, the ending of *The Golden Dog*, with its emphasis on the bizarre cage in which La Corriveau's body is left to rot and on her bones which have a lasting power over man's imagination as relics in a museum, deliberately plays upon gothic motifs. And, seemingly to ensure that the reader suffers a concluding stroke of terror, Kirby draws attention to life's incomprehensibility, stating that 'there is neither human nor poetic justice' in it.

Kirby's double insistence in *The Golden Dog* upon realistic, historical details and gothic motifs is the clue to its main weakness. If *The Golden Dog* has interest in the externals as historical details, then the gothic additions clutter an already highly romantic tale. Even without the gothic motifs, the story would be sufficiently lively and exotic to justify Frye's comment on the book, that

the forlorn little fortress to seventeenth-century Quebec, sitting in the middle of what Madame de Pompadour called "a few arpents of snow," acquires a theatrical glamour that would do credit to Renaissance Florence.[3]

Conversely, if *The Golden Dog* was written as a gothic expression of the darker side of life, then it fails since, as Kirby's concluding statement indicates, he is more inclined to tell of terror than to invoke it. Despite the gothic trappings, a sense of optimism and secure goodness overcomes the suggestion of terror; sentimentality, even when we take into account the attitudes of the age in which the story was written, subdues the superficial shudder. The dominant mood in the book is one of sentimental love. The scenes between Amélie and Pierre are obviously sweetened with sentiment. And true to the sentimental taboo about explicit sexuality, discussed earlier with reference to *Wacousta*, Amélie really only receives the kiss of death, although Pierre is finally permitted contact with her wan countenance in the convent. Amélie is another of those pristine creatures too good for this world, and the modern reader is excused for wishing her an earlier departure.

The only real feeling of demonic darkness in *The Golden Dog* comes in those moments of dreaming or introspection by Angélique. In an early nightmare, she feels herself 'falling down unfathomable abysses,' her couch 'surrounded with indefinite shapes of embryo evil.' Later she finds herself in 'a world of guilty thoughts and unresisted temptations, a chaotic world where black, unscalable rocks, like a circle of the *Inferno* hemmed her on every side.' After the death of Caroline, it seemed to Angélique

as if the lights had all gone out in the palaces and royal halls, where her imagination had so long run riot, and she saw only dark shadows and heard inarticulate sounds of strange voices babbling in her ear. (p 222)

Nevertheless these moments are brief. For the most part in *The Golden Dog*, evil seems more a source of titillation than a fearsome reality.

One reason why traditional gothic motifs seem in *The Golden Dog* ornamental props which have no truly affecting power is that they are not naturalized, but are foreign motifs. On the face of it, this assertion may seem strange in view of the indigenous roots of most of Kirby's plot. Kirby received the impetus for his tale from James Le Moine's *Maple Leaves*,[4] a collection of old legends and tales of Quebec. As Kirby relates,

I was so captivated by the dramatic interest infused into two out of the several sketches it contained, *Chateau Bigot* and *The Golden Dog*, that I vowed to a friend, I would make them the groundwork of a Canadian novel. Thus originated my Chien d'Or romance.[5]

Gothic images, however, are symbolic. Charles Brockden Brown was the first North American gothic writer to substitute the haunted forest and the cave or pit for the ruined castle and dungeon, a change in myth which Fiedler maintains involves a change in meaning beyond the substitute of different, picturesque effects:

In the American gothic ... the heathen, unredeemed wilderness and not the decaying monuments of dying class, nature and not society becomes the symbol of evil. Similarly not the aristocrat but the Indian, not the dandified courtier but the savage coloured man is postulated as the embodiment of evil.[6]

Although, as discussed in the analysis of *Wacousta*, Canadian experience involves a complex and unresolved duality of awe and fear in regard to both nature and sophisticated society, Canadians, like Americans, are more aroused by the menace of nature symbolized by the forest than by the menace of the past symbolized by the haunted castle.

Fiedler describes the traditional European motifs of crumbling castle and shadowy corridors, pursued heroine and pursuing villain, as symbolic embodiments of 'the guilt of the revolutionary haunted by the (paternal) past which he has been trying to destroy.'[7] If the nineteenth-century European writer

permitted himself a certain relish in the contemplation of those ruins, this was because they were safely cast down and he could indulge in nostalgia without risk. If he was terrified of them, dreamed supernatural enemies lurking in their shadows, it was because he suspected that the past, even dead, *especially* dead, could continue to work harm.[8]

Although some critics differ from Fiedler as to the nature of the revolt – for example, Varma claims that the gothic romance records 'a revolt against the oppressive materialism of the time'[9] – many more critics agree that the images of European gothic fiction are essentially revolutionary in spirit.

Thus despite their position in French-Canadian history, Bigot and his chateau as *symbols* did not have a real potential for terror for the French Canadian of the nineteenth century. Still bound in spirit to traditional authority, the dominant attitude of French Canada was conservative, not revolutionary. Kirby shares this attitude. As a result, the aristocratic ghosts of the past could not really haunt or terrify with the same force as could the symbolic threat of the forest or the Indian. Still it is possible, considering the impact of the 'Quiet Revolution' in Quebec, that the cluster of images surrounding the crumbling castle would have more gothic potential for the mid-twentieth-century, French Canadian than for that of the last century.

One might assume nonetheless that at least La Corriveau would work as a gothic image, since she has such a prominent place in French-Canadian legend. Yet I think that Kirby's witch does not really fulfil the traditional role. In *The Golden Dog*, as mentioned earlier, she represents the manipulative intelligence and its inhumane possibilities; this is not nearly as culturally threatening as the more pure spiritual evil she represents in Aubert de Gaspé's rendition.[10] In *Les Anciens Canadiens*, she must overcome the powers of God at work in the prescribed church ritual of the blessing of the St Lawrence River. In Kirby's romance, La Corriveau's *knowledge* offers satisfaction to Angélique's lust for power, and therefore is victor over the latter's softer, more humane impulses.

Since the gothic elements in *The Golden Dog* do not effectively represent profound inner anxieties or fears, they are merely melodramatic colouring. The reader can respond to this tale of thrills and chills with a certain detachment; he is sometimes apt to smile rather than to take it seriously.

Thus there is a fundamental difference between *The Golden Dog* and *Wacousta*. While both have adopted many conventional gothic motifs, Kirby has not adapted them as successfully to the Canadian experience. While both Kirby and Richardson build upon historical incidents, these have been utilized to different effect. Although in *Wacousta* there is less realistic detail than in *The Golden Dog*, the fantasy or romance of the central story does not so much transport us from real life as attempt to bring us face to face with it in all its difficult aspects. The historical surface is timeless because it expresses an inward reality which still has meaning for us.

The Golden Dog, despite its obvious attention to details of history and geography, presents life with a drop of faked bitters and a spoonful of sugar. Despite its overlay of conventional images of horror, Kirby's romance does not confront the problematic or ambiguous in life, but rather it supplies a comfortable cushion from which one can vicariously enjoy the exotic adventures of another time while resting secure and assured. Like so many lesser works which preceded and followed it, the gothicism in *The Golden Dog* is decorative rather than truly functional.

4

Towards the Grotesque:
Le Chercheur de trésors

In his preface to *Le Chercheur de trésors*,[1] initially called *L'Influence d'un livre*, Philippe Aubert de Gaspé (fils) asserts his realistic and historical purpose; namely that he is presenting the country's first Canadian novel of manners:

J'ai décrit les événements tels qu'ils sont arrivés, n'en tenant presque toujours à la réalité, persuadé qu'elle doit toujours remporter l'avantage sur la fiction la mieux ourdie. Le Canada, pays, vierge encore dans son enfance, n'offre aucun des ces grands caractères qui ont fourni un champ si vaste au genre des romanciers de la vieille Europe. Il a donc fallu ne contenter de peindre des hommes tels qu'ils se rencontient dans la vie usuelle. Mareuil et Amand font seuls les exceptions: le premier par sa soif du sang humain; la second, par sa folie innocente. (p 2)

Such an insistence upon actuality reminds one of Richardson's apology for the two geographic inaccuracies of *Wacousta*, and is no less misleading. Aubert de Gaspé's romance is not a realistic portrait of Quebec. Rather, his supposed depiction of 'la vie usuelle' is a singular vision of life perceived through the coloured lens of his own emotions and imagination, a vision in which the flickering reds of passion and violent energy fight against the darker hues of encroaching despair. *Le Chercheur de trésors* is as much the internal countryside of Aubert de Gaspé's own anxious spirit as the external country shared by his compatriots.

This emphasis on subjective reality obviously does not deny the factual basis of many of the incidents, any more than it denies the historical veracity of the background in *Wacousta*. Several critics have been at pains to trace the correspondence of certain episodes and characters to actual records.[2] There are also some realistic depictions of the habits and décor of Quebec living, notably in the scenes of rustic gatherings. Nevertheless, for Aubert de Gaspé as for Richardson, the essential truth of their stories is psychological; the narrative details are in many instances symbolic manifestations of spiritual or cultural difficulties for which there is no easy solution.

The first paragraph of the book gives evidence of a *paysage intérieur*. We are not directed to a specific locale, but learn only that the hero's cabin is on the south bank of the St Lawrence near a chain of mountains 'dont nous ignorons le nom.' This deliberate imprecision suggests the irrelevance of regional particularity in the vision the author is trying to present.

In some ways the *paysage intérieur* is equally imprecise in its directions. Despite the symbolic reference given to many of the incidents and characterizations, no clear-cut moral or philosophic position emerges. *Le Chercheur de trésors* has occasionally been read as an attack upon materialism. Certainly the title of the book refers to both the gold-lust of Amand and Guillemette's motive for murder, and can also be extended as a comment upon Quebec society as a whole. Saint-Céran, in one of the book's most directly didactic sections, condemns money-grubbing society, and more especially those women in it who marry for money rather than love.

Yet if materialism were the simple object of attack, one should probably have found a more tightly structured novel. An identified evil, whether human or ideological, is normally a great unifying device in a novel. In truth, the danger of a precise evil is that it tends to make an overly directed or didactic novel, one that is forced into too narrow a mould.

Aubert de Gaspé's novel lacks such an ordering device; the narrative is loosely tied, with constant switches of focus. The characters wander in and out of view in such an unpredictable fashion that at times the book seems a house for itinerant roomers. As the story of Amand begins to gather momentum, the murder by Mareuil in the third chapter forms a long episode which diverts our attention. Moreover, in at least one case the narrative line is left dangling, never to be picked up again. The story of Madeleine's departure with a young man is never completed; the related tale of Rose Latulipe raises our suspicions about her, but we never learn of the outcome.

This apparent disunity has less to do with Aubert de Gaspé's deliberate disregard for the classical unities – although he mentions in his preface his romantic disdain for them – than with the uncertainty in his own mind over the moral direction he should take. Léopold Leblanc[3] astutely remarks that the importance of money to the central character is only an outer box over another concern – the need for recognition: 'Si Charles Amand recherche la fortune, c'est pour obtenir un peu de considération.' Amand represents the humiliation of French-Canadian culture and its extreme spiritual poverty. Leblanc sees the Québecois in *Le Chercheur de trésors* as a man without a country. As represented by Amand's wandering, and that of the hawker, the mendicant, and even Saint-Céran, he is always an 'homme de passage.' Unable to face the present, he turns in reverie to the past and the future – to the world of fantastic legend and of magic dream.

Yet while the Québecois in *Le Chercheur de trésors* is displaced or without direction, it is also apparent that Aubert de Gaspé himself is equally disoriented in a spiritual sense. He may well 'décrire la réalité québecoise' as Leblanc states, but his romance indicates his own confusion as to the needed alternative. The treasure which is desired in this story is not really the gold of Amand's dream but a set of values by which to live. Aubert de Gaspé, like Amand, seeks his own kind of philosopher's stone, with the ability to transmute the horrible reality of everyday living into a golden atmosphere of harmony and happiness. In doing so, he confronts the present confusion, relentlessly following the implication of its alternatives often right to the edge of spiritual darkness.

Le Chercheur de trésors is gothic in its imaginative awareness and exploration of lurking evils, evils which are various and pervasive and which therefore seem to prevent man from realizing a satisfactory way of life for himself. The various characters and incidents are not joined in a unified plot, but are related as symbolic revelations and refractions of a deeply-felt malaise, gothic in its proportions. At the same time the author's frustration and uncertainty about traditional values is at the centre of many of the grotesque incidents in the narrative, which mark the work as a precursor of the disruptive grotesque mode common in twentieth-century fiction.

From the first chapter, we are warned of the difficulty of establishing values and moral guidelines in a life of frustration and increasing hopelessness, and of the temptation of evil both as a means to an end and as a self-sufficient satisfaction. Faced with the humiliation and abasement of his own miserable poverty, Amand enlists the help of his friend Dumas in stealing a black hen, the necessary ingredient in his magic process of transmutation. Dumas recognizes and recoils from the sinister implications of this criminal act, guessing at the binding consequences, both spiritual and physical, of a deed which had been conceived as liberating: 'Il lui semble que l'atmosphère était plus étroite, une sueur froide coulait sur son front, et il se sentait extenue, ses jambes pouvaient à peine supporter.' Nature itself takes on a new, fearsome aspect as a harbinger of spiritual agonies: 'Chaque arbre lui semblait un fantôme, et le vent qui bruissait dans le feuillage lui semblait un gémissement qui tombait sur son esprit comme le râle de la dernière agonie d'un mourant.' Amand, however, is not deterred. Warned by Dumas that by indulging in necromancy their actions would put them 'dans la société du diable,' he rationalizes his actions as a momentary necessity, as the employment of a devilish means which he can subsequently abandon. Thwarted in his plan, he curses Dumas and plans henceforth to trust no other man than himself.

This hasty sketch of the opening episode may suggest that Amand is a heroic villain in the traditional, gothic pattern. Yet from the beginning the impotence and foolishness of his schemes puts him in ironic contrast to any gothic stance of proud defiance. Amand is a ludicrous figure, but horror or fearfulness is also connected with the accounts of his behaviour, especially when it is seen in the context of his confining circumstances and the cultural and spiritual dead end of his misguided desires. This combination of ludicrous and fearful qualities is, as we have seen, the essence of Ruskin's definition of the grotesque. The opening scene establishes the grotesque dimension of Aubert de Gaspé's story, drawing a mixed response of amusement, pity, and horror, as unsettling to the reader as the traditional gothic mood of pure terror.

The unrelievedly horrifying side of life bursts forth in the shock treatment of the second episode with its insistence upon human depravity. Mareuil's murder of the hawker is the latest of his habitual acts upon innocent victims, and it is described in all its bloody detail – the slitting of the drugged Guillemette's jugular vein, the repeated stabbing, the thud of the body on the floor, and its final descent into the river where it lies exposed on the muddy bottom. It is significant that there is no motive given for the crime other than the delight Mareuil receives in spilling blood and in the processes of killing. Mareuil seems an agent of all that is arbitrary and unjust in life and in death; at the same time he seems a constant reminder of original sin, of an evil that cannot be explained away or destroyed with rationalization, but which lies ready to cut loose in an orgy of violence and destruction. Mareuil's dream represents with its details the cancerous and ultimately isolating effects of evil and the guilt which pursues one even past the grave. In *Le Chercheur de trésors*, the millions of vermin which eat at the dreamer's cadaver are as nothing compared to torments of guilt; evil may be persistent and unpreventable, but evildoers are destroyed with their victims.

Beyond this dramatic insistence upon the presence of evil in man and society, Aubert de Gaspé examines various other aspects of Quebec life which people have turned to as a source of strength or value. Their insufficiency increases the sense of estrangement from meaning or moral order characteristic of much modern, disruptive grotesque fiction, as we shall see later, La Vieille Nollet, renowned necromancer and sorceress who is consulted by Amand, may be seen to represent the superstitions which rule the lives of ignorant people. Aubert de Gaspé deliberately contrasts her repulsive demeanour with the sentimental creation of another writer, Charles Nodier:

Elle ressemblait assez à ces magots que l'imagination vive de nos jeunes filles a placés sur leurs roues de fortune pour dicter avec leur balai, accompagnement indispensable d'une sorcière, leur succès futur. (p 54)

While La Vieille Nollet predicts the success of humans who show courage, strength, and energy, traits which are held up elsewhere as distinctive and superior human attributes, her supposedly supernatural powers are also revealed as the tricks of a charlatan when she initially overestimates the number of a man's children.

Other episodes in the novel provide a further questioning probe into the power of supernaturalism, and at times even seem to cast a shadow on the role of traditional religion itself. The framed legend of Rose Latulipe provides an illustration. In this legend one is told about a Mardi Gras celebration during which Rose Latulipe was persuaded to neglect her fiancé and promise her hand to a handsome stranger, the devil in disguise. Only the strength and courage of the parish priest is able to break this satanic bond; the devil disappears in a puff of sulphurous smoke, and Rose escapes to spend the rest of her days in a convent. Since the convent represents the spiritual life removed from the world, and therefore the only refuge from the pursuing clutches of evil, it is strange that in her escape to safety in this Christian community, Rose at the end is referred to as 'malheureuse.'

Moreover, why is the story of Rose framed by the story of Marguerite, since Duclos could just as well have directly related the legend of Rose without the intervening episode? One answer lies in the atmosphere of suspense and menace it produces. Since the story of Marguerite parallels the initial circumstances of Rose, one may feel that she also will be entrapped by Satan as her father half anticipates. Will her disregard for traditional pieties by dancing on Ash Wednesday be the beginning of her downfall, as it was for Rose? Another possible interpretation would contrast the gay companionship of Marguerite and Joseph, as they discuss their father's worries, with the 'superstitious' fears of Rose, separated from fiancé and family, as she suffers under the weight of her spiritual sin.

Related to the uncertainty or diversity of interpretation surrounding the Marguerite-Rose Latulipe episodes is the ambiguity about the image of Rose's hand, pricked by the devil and dripping blood. Does this image indicate that Rose's spiritual crime is as serious as the bloody deed of Mareuil, or is this image a deliberate parody of the conventional stigmata, suggesting the superstitious nature of both?

The ambiguity of Aubert de Gaspé's religious position is suggested in the narration of the legend of Rodrigue Bras-de-Fer. A defiant, proud figure, who feared neither God nor the devil, Bras-de-Fer had in his youth led a life of debauchery, dissipation, and eventually of murder. Finally, alone in a drunken stupor, he suffers a series of terrible apparitions, including the visit of diabolic imps and a huge satanic figure with flame-like breath, who is only put to flight through an invocation to God. This story of a diabolical visitation, told by the tormented beggar about his youth, is fully believed by Amand. Yet a student questions its validity, explaining it as a guilty hallucination of a drunk. As in the previous legend, a certain ambiguity remains. Is Armand's belief simply a superstitious folly of the ig-norant, to be equated with the naïve belief in alchemy and necromancy? In the end one is not sure whether Aubert de Gaspé regards traditional religion itself as an offspring of ignorance, an oppressive force which counteracts the natural vital-ity of the people, or whether he also is caught up in the Jansenist spirit of guilty fear and expectation of severe punishment. Certainly divine vengeance is often in the characters' thoughts and is sometimes even seen to explain the workings of nature. For example, after Mareuil's murder the thunder 'grondait comme au jugement dernier.' Saint-Céran remarks that the noise of the elements is owing to the avenging angel, but the light-hearted spirit of the conversation raises a ques-tion about his seriousness.

While the inconclusiveness of Aubert de Gaspé's religious attitude contributes to the disoriented quality of the novel, there is a more basic ambivalence, which persists from beginning to end of the book, in the contrast between natural and civilized values. In the opening chapter we are introduced to Charles Amand, a man who struggles vainly to change base metals into gold, and whose dreams pro-ject him into a world where 'il lui semble qu'il était sur un miroir d'or et de rubis et que tout cela était à lui.' Yet the description of the natural environment which closely follows provides an ironic suggestion of the superior blessings of natural living, that nature itself may be the most precious jewel available to Charles: 'Qu'il paraît riche avec ses nombreux îlots, en forme de couronne, charges de pins verts qui semblent autant d'émeraudes parsemées sur une toile d'argent.'

The contrast between natural and civilized values is more obviously repre-sented in the antipathetic attitudes and characters of the rustic Amand and the culturally educated Saint-Céran. On the one hand, Aubert de Gaspé seems to ad-mire some of Amand's natural qualities. Amand obviously fulfils La Nollet's re-quirements of stout heart, energy, and strength (see p 56), and even the conde-scending medical students admire his spirit, while reflecting 'sur le malheur de cette âme énergique qui, par son ignorance, se trouvait reduite à poursuivre toute sa vie une chimère.'

In an overtly didactic passage, thinly disguised as Saint-Céran's musings, there is, as we have seen, a condemnation of the vanity and folly of self-seeking civil-ized society and particularly of the artificiality and deception of its women. The latter respond to materialism and social pressures which 'éteint le feu naturel.' Speaking of women, Saint-Céran remarks:

Dans leur enfance, c'était un plaisir de les entendre, de les voie, de les aimer: elles étaient pures, naïves et riantes: mais la société les a bientot flétries. (p 43)

Saint-Céran excepts Amélie, the gentle child of nature, from this condemnation, and finally wins her on his return to the countryside. Significantly, Amélie remains apart from that urban life and sophisticated society which Saint-Céran is familiar with and quits.

Although materialism and the life of deception which it breeds are at the centre of Saint-Céran's condemnation, there is also a recognition in the book that the 'noble savage' often leads a life of impoverished misery, as do Amand and his poor wife. When Amand awakens from the soft glow of his dream, 'la froide réalité veut rappeler à notre héros qu'il était seul, couché sur un misérable grabat et presque mourant d'inanition au fond d'une chaumière.' The author himself asks: 'Que n'aurait pas fait cet homme si son imagination fertile eut été fécondée par l'éducation?' He also comments on the new self-confidence and sense of well-being which the possession of a little wealth and good clothes gives to Amand, that 'ces deux choses aient une influence grande sur le moral d'un homme.' Moreover, he takes pains to assure his readers that Saint-Céran and Amélie spend the rest of their days 'pleins de prospérité et de bonheur' – an interesting combination of blessings for a supposed anti-materialist!

The converse of Amand's naïve ignorance is Saint-Céran's cultivated outlook. Whereas Amand's ignorance is connected with his difficulties, the knowledge imparted by civilized society is seemingly connected with Saint-Céran's success and happiness in the affairs of life. In many instances in the book, the man of knowledge is pitted against the man of ignorance or simple, natural experience. It is a student, as we have seen, who questions the validity of the penitent woodsman's diabolical apparitions, and it is two students who, in their joking, superior way, make a fool of the treasure-hunting Amand. It is as a student also that Saint-Céran, in his letter to Amélie, remarks upon her ridiculous father and finally exposes to his future father-in-law, by reference to his scientific dictionary, the empty promise of the touted 'or piment.' Aubert de Gaspé pointedly states that it is after some period spent reflecting as a student of society that Saint-Céran discovers the faults of society.

The conflict between natural and civilized life in *Le Chercheur de trésors* reflects less a pull between opposing goods than a dispiriting realization of the final insufficiency of either as reliable ideals. Aubert de Gaspé's attitude is similar in this respect to John Richardson's, and it supports the view presented in the analysis of *Wacousta*, that a repeated characteristic of Canadian gothicism is the feeling of being caught between the opposing evils or inadequacies of nature and civilization. It is this feeling and the resulting sense of a spiritual abyss which are behind the most grotesquely gothic episode in the book. The laboratory scene is the symbolic apogée of Amand's 'natural' or primitive superstitions and of Saint-Céran's 'civilized' pursuits as a medical student. Amand's determined plan, born out of desperation in his search for gold, involves procuring a magic candle composed of the fat of a human corpse, and a *main de gloire*, that is, the hand of a hanged man. Amand's desire for a magic candle and a *main de gloire* reaches its grotesque conclusion when he snatches the desired items from under the medical students' noses and tucks them under his coat.

In this respected temple of science, one is also treated to a gruesome description of the students' behaviour and the escapades with the cadavers they are dissecting, including one whose guts they had let fall out on the street. The laboratory itself is a symbolic chamber of evil, with its skeletons of criminals strung around the walls. It is symbolically fitting that the skeleton of the murderer Mareuil is set upon a horse in a reminder of a well-known painting of the Apocalypse. Of special interest also is the recognition that this focus on cadavers and on disfigurement prefigures an emphasis in later twentieth-century French-Canadian fiction. What Aubert de Gaspé expresses in this scene is his sense of darkness and horror in both antithetical attitudes; Amand's 'natural' superstition and Saint-Céran's 'civilized' scientific knowledge are ultimately disintegrating, destructive, or inhuman in their effects, as symbolized in the treatment of the human corpse. Their focus may also be a reminder of the death-in-life existence of the characters, a common motif in gothic and grotesque fiction, or alternately it may indicate that all human aspirations, whatever diverse route they follow, are tainted by the smell of death.

Le Chercheur de trésors reveals that Aubert de Gaspé was often close to despair in his view of life. In his conclusion, however, he seems to have recoiled a step back from the spiritual chasm he was exposing. Or he may simply have tried a desperate last move to provide a solution. In any case, the ending of the book, like the ending of *Wacousta*, provides a rather artificial synthesis or reconciliation of opposing attitudes, and points sentimentally to a satisfying future. The two main characters each alter their former ways, supposedly gaining from the opposing side the missing ingredient in a happy existence. Saint-Céran abandons the city for the country and leaves behind his scientific studies, that is, his pursuit of objective knowledge, to return to the world of literature, the realm of imaginative reality or fantasy which Amand in another way has formerly participated in. Amand, on the other hand, begins a serious study of scientific books given him by Saint-Céran. Yet it is the *science* of nature which will continue to preoccupy him, a seeming synthesis of contrasting values.

Despite the supposed solution provided by the ending, the work essentially is a troubled one. Even in the comic passages, in which the behaviour of Amand has a ridiculous aspect, there is a rueful undertone to the mirth. Although Amand is the butt of his own foolishness, as when he falls into the trap of the gleeful students, he is also a victim of life, trapped in circumstances from which he can never really escape. But more important, he is trapped in the narrowness of his own vision and thus deformed by it; he is a grotesque. If Amand's life is a joke, it is black humour, a laugh in the dark in which the threatening face of annihilating personal and social evils looms into view.

Le Chercheur de trésors provides an early Canadian example of the tragicomic mélange so often observed as the prominent feature of twentieth-century writing. As Thomas Mann points out:

I feel that, broadly and essentially, the striking feature of modern art is that it has ceased to recognize the categories of tragic and comic, or the dramatic classifications, tragedy and comedy. It sees life as tragicomedy, with the result that the grotesque is its most genuine style.[4]

Aubert de Gaspé himself may suggest the mixed tragicomic mood of his work in the comments he gives to Saint-Céran, as the latter's friends jokingly discuss the fate of the murderer: 'Ceci n'est point matière à badinage, et le malheureux, teint du sang de son frère, doit inspirer une pitié melée d'horreur plutôt que des plaisanteries.'

Thus *Le Chercheur de trésors* is an important book for us to know as students of Canadian literature, not so much as an early attempt to depict manners and customs, but as an early gothic romance which moves towards the grotesque emphasis of much modern fiction. Aubert de Gaspé exposes with symbolic force the false hopes of many accepted attitudes and values in his day. The gothic aspect of his vision, frequently expressed in many grotesque incidents, is related to the spiritual and cultural abyss he sees at the end of these false hopes, an abyss not unlike that exposed in *Wacousta*. As we shall find later, many of the patterns he traces and the methods he uses are repeated and developed in the French-Canadian works of our time.

5

Gothic Propaganda:
For My Country: Pour la patrie

Patriotic sentiment and renewed pride in the heroic actions of the past shaped much of the literature of French Canada in the decades following Garneau's romantic rendition of history.[1] Considering the prevalent nostalgia for former glories in nineteenth-century French-Canadian romances, one is initially surprised to find that the plot of J.-P. Tardivel's *For My Country: Pour la patrie*[2] looks forward to the future rather than backward. Published in 1895, the story takes place fifty years later in 1945, a device which at the least provides some amusing moments for the contemporary reader.

The story centres upon a political crisis over the future of Quebec. Canada has just been granted from Britain its total independence as a republic, and thus Quebec, through its parliamentary representatives in Ottawa, must decide between three political options – the status quo of confederation; a legislative union, and its subsequent assimilation or downgrading of the French language and religion; and separation. The author's favour lies obviously with the third course as the necessary and only means of preserving the unity of French Canada and of restoring the Roman Catholic religion to its former, supreme status.

The hero of the novel, Dr Joseph Lamirande, is a devout Catholic and a French-Canadian patriot. As a member of parliament, he attempts to defeat the government's constitutional plan, a plan which in reality would be a step towards legislative union. At the head of the government is Sir Henry Marwood, a wily and unscrupulous *anglais* who Lamirande eventually discovers to be a member of the Freemasons and thus part of a plot to destroy the Roman Catholic Church. In the end the government bill is defeated, but not before Lamirande makes a bargain with St Joseph to sacrifice his ailing wife's life – with her approval – in return for the triumph of the French-Canadian patriots. As Tardivel explains, 'It is not often that a woman can save her country by dying!'

As suggested by the preceding quotation, Tardivel's hortatory fervour frequently overcomes his literary sensibility, with the result that at times the book seems little more than a zealous religious and political tract. Nevertheless the story fits into a discussion of gothicism by reason of the role assumed by the 'enemies.' While *For My Country* is concerned with society, it has little interest in analysis of everyday manners or morals, but attempts to dramatize what the author sees as a fundamental threat to the peace and serenity of French-Canadian life. As with so many other gothic works, Tardivel's romance attempts to make the menace of evil a dramatic and emotionally coloured presence in the story. Evil is at time an active agent, even personified, as in the case of the strange appearance of Eblis. However, unlike the other gothic works discussed in this section, *For My Country* uses gothic motifs and machinery as rhetoric to achieve a practical end. By appealing to emotion, it attempts to persuade the reader to fear and despise certain social groups and conversely to defend others, an attempt which places it in a special category of gothic fiction, that of gothic propaganda.

As is typical in French-Canadian, gothic writing, evil becomes identified with a danger to the established order. But whereas we are accustomed in many instances to see evil depicted by some representation from the past, be it from folk legend or historical encounters with Indian or English enemies, evil in *For My Country* is most clearly associated with the contemporary menace of the Freemasons. Freemasonry (and to a lesser degree the secular school) is seen as an instrument of the devil and a form of devil worship; its practitioners are Luciferians, who call up satanic spirits to aid in their diabolic anti-Christian designs. Descriptions of the Masons' activities are hardly realistic, but replete with conventional gothic trappings designed to raise feelings of terror.

Despite the story's setting in the future and its scientific and political projections, the novel is not really a genuine excursion into science fiction; rather, the date is a device by which a contemporary threat to the society may be heightened and expanded to gothic proportions, increasing the terror of the menace without jeopardizing its case by any exact comparison with existing conditions, or with contemporary politicians. Tardivel distances the story from the present in order to intensify its effect on the present. In doing so, he pulls out all the gothic stops within reach of his tale and the reader's credibility. Aside from the satanic seances of the Freemasons, there is a modernized twist to the traditional murder by poison, in which Marie Lamirande appears to succumb to the effects of a deadly virus. A traditional, gothic besetting-and-chase routine focuses principally upon Ducoudray, enemy and spy of Lamirande until his sudden conversion from Freemasonry to Roman Catholicism. Ducoudray himself is subsequently followed, until he is stabbed to death on a dark sidewalk by the mysterious man in dark glasses, who acts under orders from the Grand Mason.

The arch-villain of the tale, the diabolic, anti-Christian schemer, Montarval, whose inhumanity is first seen in his callous desertion of his poor father, is given a lurid death scene in the gothic mould. Mortally wounded by a self-inflicted shot in the head, 'His breathing was only a rattle, and from his right temple a thin stream of blood spilled, drop by drop, onto the floor. His eyes were open, glassy and staring.' Suddenly a colossal, devilish form takes shape out of the mist, which 'froze the blood in their veins'; Montarval utters a cry of anger at this deceiving Eblis and after a final expression of hatred toward God, 'a convulsive tremor shook him from head to foot' and he dies.

Yet neither here nor elsewhere in the book is the reader at one with those characters who experience 'faces white with terror ... flesh trembling and afraid.' For every gothic depiction of the forces of evil, Tardivel creates a sentimental counter in which virtue and goodness are triumphant, a pattern similar to that in *Wacousta*, and typical of much nineteenth-century fiction. Not only are Montarval and his allies routed, but all the essentially 'good' characters are at the end safe and together in the folds of Mother Church. The agnostic Vaughan, about whom Tardivel pointedly remarks that 'He had been inculcated with the poison of incredulity in his childhood, in the public schools of his province,' had even in his skepticism looked favourably on the Catholic faith. He remarks that 'if there is something true in any religion, it is in the Catholic faith.' In the end Vaughan is converted by the spiritual example of Lamirande and achieves a new nobility. Houghton, impressed by the change in Vaughan, is likewise converted. No spiritual stone is left unturned; no virtue, it would seem, may reside for long outside the faith. Even the final satanic spectre, which surfaces at the death-bed bidding of Montarval, is surpassed by the final death scene of the saintly Lamirande, when a heavenly harmony and perfume herald the appearance of his dead young daughter Marie, sent from heaven to fetch him to God. The miracles and *dénouement* of the story are designed to show that Lamirande is the instrument of a new destiny for French Canadians – that political separation and the supremacy of the true Church are God's choice for Quebec.

Even the bleak and often bitter realities of winter weather are softened and worked into the religious design. The snow which descends upon the streets of Quebec is an 'image of divine mercy that sheds an immaculate garment over the ugliness of the soul that transgresses but is repentant.' Yet one notices that the murder of Marie Lamirande is indirectly precipitated by a snowstorm which halts the train – an unintended instance of irony which by its isolation must be considered an unconscious didactic lapse rather than an artistic subtlety.

As one might suspect at this point, the greatest 'frisson' experienced from *Fo My Country* is connected not with the terrifying events as much as with the author's philosophy and attitude. Tougas has remarked upon the 'racist' and bigote nature of this book,[3] a book which, incidentally, was widely bestowed until r cently as a prize for school children in Quebec. No non-Catholic is trustworthy, the bishop tells Lamirande, since the 'true faith is the necessary basis for all true good.' Even the skeptical Vaughan dismisses Protestantism with the explanation that a good religion cannot issue from an impure source and only the Catholic religion has a founder worthy of respect. Such religious or nationalistic biases are nothing new to fiction. Yet they are potentially a greater harm to the artistic merit of a romance than to that of a novel of manners and morals. The romance requires a higher degree of emotional and unanalytic commitment from the reader, a 'willing suspension of disbelief' which is diminished by a critical or unsympathetic reaction.

Moreover for a gothic novel to produce a genuine shudder the powers of darkness are best represented as essentially mysterious or boundless. Thus the embodiment of evil must be a symbolic as well as a particular threat, and the villain a manifestation of some greater menace, if it is to be truly terrifying. One realizes, for example, that while the Indians are an actual threat in North American gothic romances, their greater force is as a symbol of irrationality or human savagery. A different kind of symbolic meaning is repeatedly given to the licentious aristocrat in European gothicism, as Fiedler has pointed out. Tardivel, on the other hand, has chosen to define his evil as Freemasonry. He has given it explicit boundaries and a specific sociological place by emphasizing the daily political scene and the educational and religious issues surrounding it. By this emphasis on the actual, he has shrunk or restricted the symbolic possibilities, and thus forced the reader to assess the content of the evil in the context of everyday, social awareness. When seen in this light by the contemporary reader, the menace is as laughable as the panacea is questionable.

In another way, the characterization of the central hero of the book also serves to modify or counteract the gothic effect of *For My Country* as a whole. We are accustomed in gothic romances to find a black-and-white characterization with little of the motley, greyish shades appropriate to common mortality. Nevertheless, in most instances, the sense of fanatic purpose or obsession is reserved mainly for the villain, whose loss of humanity is to some extent associated with this extremism or obstinate zeal. The hero or heroine, if either there be, is by comparison more variable, hesitant, or temperate in practice even if he or she has spun gold ideals.

In his preface, Tardivel states that novels are weapons 'forged by Satan,' but he acknowledges the condition under which novelists should use those weapons: 'We must be certain that we know how to handle the devices without wounding our own troops.' Ironically and unfortunately, Tardivel has in fact wounded his own troops by adopting the devil's habit and manner for his hero. In *For My Country* the villainous Montarval is obsessed by his anti-Christian hatred. Similarly the lesser villain, Prime Minister Marwood, is not simply a self-interested prag-matist, but acts under the rule of 'the God of Liberty, Progress, and Vengeance' – the latter hardly a political or philosophical principle but a rather common, gothic motive. Yet neither of these men matches in intensity the zealous fervour of Lamirande, whose obsessive mission makes the choice whether to save his wife or his cause a rather quick decision. The single-minded purpose of the hero serves to diminish the horror of the single-minded villain; the terrifying aspect of Mont-arval is reduced by the counteracting force of his mirror opposite. Since 'inhu-man' drive and obsessive energy cannot by itself suggest a satanic quality, the moral position must be established by critical differentiation between the right-ness and wrongness of their beliefs, that is, by forcing once again a reaction to the content of their beliefs rather than the quality of their responses.

Tardivel no doubt intended to stage a massive battle between the forces of good and of evil. As Father Grandmont emphasizes: 'it is impossible to be neutral, a simple spectator. One must choose one side or the other; 'march with Christ or towards Hell under Lucifer's flag.' Tardivel clearly hoped to inflame passions for the cause of faith and country by raising the terrifying vision of satanic forces ready to annihilate the race. While these gothic forces need not have been victor-ious, they should have been more dominant if he was to achieve his emotional purpose. In not making them more dominant, Tardivel limited success of his work as a propaganda piece as much as he limited its artistic merit as gothic fiction.

Yet despite its obvious weakness, *For My Country* merits inclusion in any dis-cussion of early gothic romances in its depiction of the spectres roused in the French-Canadian psyche of lurking terrors outside the charmed circle of tradi-tional religious beliefs. Tardivel reveals to us a Quebec version of the garrison cul-ture, and expresses, albeit crudely at times, a genuine fear of impending menace and possible collapse of the culture. Tardivel's attempt at gothic propaganda fails, partially by making the terrifying unknown into an accessible and therefore easily conquerable known. Nevertheless, he at least makes tracks on a path followed and extended by a number of French-Canadian writers, whose gothicism is also asso-ciated with a pressing, spiritual anxiety.

PART TWO

TWENTIETH-CENTURY GOTHIC FICTION

6

Modern Gothic

To describe the modern era as a time of profound change and disorder, and of confused and collapsing values, is to flourish the obvious. That the undermining of established ideas and beliefs has created widespread and sustained anxiety in present generations is also a familiar story. It should not be surprising, then, that this anxiety has been related to the kind of literature twentieth-century writers have created – to the growing wave of gothic fiction, particularly of the grotesque variety.

Despite the problems involved in connecting literary forms or modes to history, the relationship between the grotesque and periods of cultural disorder or upheaval has been discussed by several critics. Kayser maintains that the grotesque mode is especially prevalent in three historical periods, 'the sixteenth century, the age which extends from the *Sturm und Drang* to Romanticism, and the twentieth century. In these periods the belief of the preceding ages in a perfect protective natural order ceased to exist.'[1] Lewis Lawson seconds Kenneth Burke's statement that 'the grotesque comes to the fore when confusion in the forensic pattern (cultural frame of reality) gives more prominence to the subjective elements of imagery than to the objective, or public, elements.'[2]

A distinction is sometimes made between the cultural climate tending to favour the creation of the grotesque and that favouring the more general category of gothic literature. Kayser suggests that whereas the grotesque presents an absurd world, eighteenth-century gothic literature presents an order which is menaced but not yet collapsed. He admits, however, that gothic, horror literature of the 1920s has a radically abysmal quality, which attempts to demolish the middle class world view rather than become integrated with it. Yet despite the difficulty in establishing conditions conducive to grotesque as opposed to gothic literature, there appears to be some special correlation between the grotesque, with its exaggerated distortions and bizarre juxtapositions, and the confused and often extremist social and cultural climate of our times.

The general upsurge of gothic and grotesque elements in the literature of modern Europe and the United States is also evident in twentieth-century Canadian fiction. It is especially persistent in the recent writing of French Canada, just as in the United States it occurs most frequently in the American South. Why these two areas show a particular predilection for the gothic and the grotesque warrants some attention and speculation.

The first possible reason has to do with their common experience of defeat. For French Canadians, the defeat by the English in the campaigns of 1754-63, like the Civil War for the American South, remains the great tragedy and central crisis of their history. Lawson's description of the aftermath of the battle in the United States is equally applicable to Quebec: 'The effect of the war was so great that the modern southern mind has been obsessed with history ... and with what might be called a mystique of defeat.'[3] One consequence of the preoccupation with defeat is a frame of mind less disposed to optimism and an easy faith in inevitable progress than is found in other sectors of American and Canadian society. French-Canadian literature, like that of the American South, centres on the losers, the loners, the monstrous cripples, and the victims of the world – subjects especially suited to the grotesque mode of writing.[4]

Paradoxically perhaps, the fact of physical defeat in both societies led in the postwar years to a stronger sense of cultural unity. Both French Canada and the American South for many years rallied around the idea of themselves as a beseiged minority threatened by an outside menace – the Anglais and the Yankee; the theme obviously has gothic overtones. However, in the twentieth century the menace has acquired a technological focus. French Canada, like the American South, traditionally has seen itself as an agrarian society, with longstanding agrarian values which conflict dramatically with the new industrialism. Throughout the years, the sacredness of the soil and rural life in general assumed the proportions of a cultural myth. The historical and economic fact became a doctrine: the old way must be maintained as a key to cultural survival. The onrush of technological change in both such conservative societies has had a cataclysmic effect on the old ideals and institutions, with the result that there has been a more overwhelming sense of doom, estrangement, and confusion than in other areas of North America. This provides another possible reason why the gothic and grotesque theme of disintegration, both of a social and a personal kind, has dominated much of their writing.

Still another similarity between French Canada and the American South, which may have contributed to a concentration of grotesque literature, is the persistent, spiritual emphasis. The power of religion in what is often called the Bible Belt long equalled the power if not the institutional authority of the Church in Quebec. The Calvinist and fundamentalist influence of the former, like the

Jansenist attitude in Quebec,[5] produced a greater awareness and fear of human evil than was felt by many of the more liberal or humanistic religious attitudes of other groups in the United States and Canada – although in the case of Canada, Calvinism obviously had a strong hold throughout the country. In recent times the influence of religion has been undermined, and in Quebec there has been a marked reaction against it. Yet despite the increased unconcern or antipathy towards matters explicitly religious, Quebec still shares with the South an undiminished concern with evil. A sense of man's natural corruption or depravity remains strong. Despite some recent Marxist inroads, there has not been a widespread acceptance of economic determinism or even of the psychological determinism underlying much modern thought. The anxiety or concern expressed by writers in these two areas is still most likely to be spiritual anxiety.

Consequently, in Quebec as in the American South there remains a fundamental choice; man does not yet live in an amoral world, but can decide between good and evil. The implications for literature have been clearly stated: 'If there is still choice, there is still evil to be warned against; hence comes one of the reasons for the grotesque.'[6] Nevertheless, while the exaggerated expression of evil found in grotesque literature reflects essentially a religious outlook, as Ruskin, Hassan, and others have pointed out, it often has a social context. The warning contained in grotesque distortion may be associated with the evil of new social attitudes and ideas or with elements of the old order which have 'gone bad.'

Moreover since popular, scientific dogmas have not been substituted for religion as yet, there remains a basic acceptance of nature's inscrutability and the mystery inherent in life. As Lawson points out, the acceptance of the inscrutability of nature allows the writer 'more freedom than his more "realistic" American counterpart; he is freer to mix real and unreal to achieve the grotesque mode. If he does not know the bounds of reality, he explores and, by that action, widens them.'[7] Grotesque fiction of Quebec and the South basically presents a view of the world as mysterious and of man as its chief riddle.

Although the major portion of modern gothic fiction is grotesque, some can really only be called gothic; Anne Hébert's *Kamouraska*, Martha Ostenso's *Wild Geese*, and Margaret Atwood's *Surfacing* are examples of modern gothic works in which the grotesque is not a dominant feature.

Within grotesque fiction, it is possible to make a distinction between that which is disruptive and that which is directed.[8] Disruptive grotesque fiction generally flouts conventional attitudes or beliefs and deliberately shocks, but has a sense of anarchical dissatisfaction rather than positive purpose; it lacks an overall moral or philosophic direction. It is the type of grotesque to which most contemporary French-Canadian writers are inclined, as *La Guerre, Yes Sir!* and *Mad Shadows* exemplify.

On the other hand, in directed grotesque fiction the fantasy has a practical end; that is, it points to a moral or philosophic framework. Fantastic satire, such as the burlesque and distorted caricatures in Mordecai Richler's *Cocksure*, is directed, as is the symbolic fantasy of Sheila Watson's *The Double Hook* and Leonard Cohen's attempt at mysticism in *Beautiful Losers*.

While English-Canadian writers, unlike their French-Canadian counterparts, have tended towards the directed grotesque fiction, it would be simplistic to come to any quick conclusions based on socio-cultural differences between the two groups. Moreover, despite the discussion of attitudes in Quebec and the American South in the last few pages, my primary interest is not sociological but generic; what follows in the next chapters is an exploration of a number of works illustrative of the basic varieties of modern gothic fiction in Canada.

Psychological Gothic: *Kamouraska*

Anne Hébert's *Kamouraska*[1] is especially suited to begin an analysis of twentieth-century gothic fiction in Canada, since in form and content it provides the reader with a double perspective, a Janus-like look both towards past and present types of gothicism. Looking one way we can see it as a continuation of the traditional black romance, with many of the gothic features and motifs of its eighteenth- and nineteenth-century predecessors. Looking another way we see it has characteristics which are undeniably contemporary and which place it in the mainstream of modern gothic writing.

Kamouraska is really a story within a story, and it is this feature in particular which lends the book to a consideration and comparison of traditional and modern gothicism. The inner story is the tale of the young Elisabeth d'Aulnières, who is married at sixteen to the brutish young squire of Kamouraska, Antoine Tassy, and forced to put up with his alcoholic violence, sadistic threats, and humiliating public affairs with women of the town, while bearing his sons. Seeing in the young doctor, George Nelson, a chance for her own passionate fulfilment and for escape from her husband, she uses her wiles to bring the servant girl, Aurélie Caron, and Nelson into a conspiracy of murder. After the bloody murder is discovered and Nelson flees to the United States, Elisabeth is herself captured, tried, imprisoned, and finally released.

Even stated with such bareness, the story clearly provides many of the ingredients of the traditional gothic romance: here are violence and bloody murder, flight, escape and imprisonment, sadism and sexuality, secrecy, trickery, and betrayal – and overall an atmosphere of fear, suspense, and explosive passion. Moreover, as in *Wacousta*, *The Golden Dog*, and many other nineteenth-century gothic romances, the story is based on an actual historical event while quickly moving into imaginative and more symbolic territory. It uses history as a starting point rather than constant reference, and makes a highly selective use of background details which are chosen for their contribution to the atmosphere or emotional impression. We learn nothing about Elisabeth's two children by Tassy except that she gave birth to them; her feelings as a young mother are not explored. The events and details which *are* given invariably seem to suggest the darker side of life. There is not a drop of sentiment anywhere. Even those brief scenes of childhood happiness have foreboding hints. For example, we catch an auspicious glimpse of Elisabeth hastily removing and hopping over her white communion dress, just as she later hops indifferently over constraining spiritual and moral matters.

Although the events of the inner story are similar to countless black romances of the last two centuries, the presence of an outer frame gives the recounting a distinctly modern cast. The tale of young Elisabeth is presented in the form of reminiscences by an older Elisabeth, now Madame Rolland, as she awaits the death of her second husband. Thus the whole novel is given as a first-person narrative, using a stream-of-consciousness technique that puts an emphasis on inner thoughts and the reaction to events as much as on the events themselves. The technique permits the inner anxieties and conflicting impulses which motivate Elisabeth to come to the fore; there is obviously a far greater attempt to get beneath the skin and perceive the psychology of the character than is found in traditional gothic romances. The use of the interior monologue heightens the subjective colouring by allowing the feelings associated with past events to impinge upon the present, and conversely by allowing present attitudes and awareness to reshape the reminiscences of the past. As Elisabeth stands her dutiful watch by her dying husband's bedside, or slumps exhausted and overwrought on the servant girl's bed, haunting memories come back to her, weaving in and out of present concerns. The face of Léontine Melançon merges with that of the earlier Aurélie Caron, just as the houses in Sorel and Kamouraska come together.

Despite the intermingling of past and present throughout *Kamouraska*, a distinction can be made between the focus in the traditionally gothic, inner story and the more modern, psychological emphasis of the outer frame, a distinction which allows us to see more clearly a difference between the two varieties. Like so many traditional gothic romances, the tale of the young Elisabeth is painted on a large and vivid canvas, full of high adventure. Even though the story is formally distanced by the device of retrospective recounting, there is still a great deal of external action which gives the tale its own momentum. The story sweeps in rapid succession from one incident to the next and from town to town, bypassing months and years as it builds in suspense to the climactic murder.

By contrast the story of Elisabeth Rolland has no really dramatic events. In fact there is little external action at all. The focus is narrowed to the world of the house on Rue du Parloir and to the small details of the domestic scene, where time is measured out as painstakingly as the drops of medicine on the lump of sugar. Where Madame Tassy fears the actual violence and physical attacks of her husband, Madame Rolland braces herself against Jérôme Rolland's subtle accusations and insinuations.

The scaling down from the large, melodramatic adventure is typical of much modern gothic writing which attempts to reveal the horror in the apparently everyday – in what seems initially to be a fairly commonplace scene. For example, where Flannery O'Connor's short stories often have a startling conclusion, they begin with such seemingly routine occurrences as a family outing ('A Good Man is Hard to Find'), or the arrival of immigrant domestic help ('Displaced Persons'). This shift in focus obviously does not involve a decrease in the atmosphere of menace and terror; the change is in the source rather than the quality of the fear.

Despite the difference in focus between large, melodramatic events and domestic commonplaces, Hébert cleverly interrelates the two stories by common images. The view from the window is used to emphasize Elisabeth's situation both as the young and the older woman. Moreover, it is symbolically important, since it accentuates the distinction between social conventions, as represented by life inside the house, and the personal freedom which beckons from outside its confines. This variation of a rather common gothic image, similar to the window treatment in *Wuthering Heights*, is a recurring motif in French-Canadian literature, to be discussed later.

At the novel's beginning, we see the older Madame Rolland looking out through the slats in the window of her husband's bedroom. The noise of the horse and wagon below recalls her earlier affair, but at this point she shrinks from its implications, deliberately closing the shutter on the window and on the passionate imaginings so removed from her conventional social role. As a young woman, however, when Elisabeth Tassy spies the doctor stopping outside her window at night, her recognition of the romantic implications ignites the spark of their illicit affair. It is fitting that, in deciding to scorn social disapproval, the lovers should stand naked before a curtainless window, as if to refute the barrier between personal desires and social dictates.

There are other, more basic similarities between the inner and outer stories, similarities which cannot simply be ascribed to the narrating personality which dominates both. They also indicate the continuity of certain gothic features, whether in the old style of narrative adventure or in the modern, psychological style.

In both stories in the novel, the demands of society are set against the demands of the irrational, passionate, or instinctive side of human nature. Although each side of the conflict has its attraction, the novel pointedly stresses the threatening or negative side of both. This sense of a double menace from both society and 'natural' man is, as we have seen in *Wacousta* and *Le Chercheur de trésors*, a repeated characteristic of Canadian gothicism. In most of the nineteenth-century gothic romances, certain individuals represent by behaviour or attitude one or another of the conflicting sides. Thus in *Wacousta* Colonel de Haldimar represents civilization and Wacousta is the irrational or natural man; in *Le Chercheur de trésors* Saint-Céran represents civilized, rational society whereas Amand represents primitive life. In *Kamouraska,* however, the double menace becomes internalized, so that within the psyche there are conflicting forces. Anne Hébert's characterization of Elisabeth places her firmly in the modern psychological pattern, as William Van O'Connor describes it: 'For the modern creator of the grotesque, man is an inextricable tangle of rationality, irrationality, love and hatred, self-improvement and self-destruction.'[2]

In Elisabeth's personality, the old conflict between civilized society and natural man may be seen in Freudian terms as conflicting claims of superego and id, a conflict in which both sides carry the threat of doom. The young Elisabeth obviously allows the id to rule over the demands of the superego, that is, she chooses the way of passion rather than of respectability. Recoiling from the cold rationalizations and propriety of her mother-in-law, she proclaims: 'I'll play out my madness to the very end. It's something I have to do. I'm on my way.' As she plunges headlong into her illicit affair with George Nelson and plots the murder of her husband against all social and moral injunctions, passionate love becomes an obsession with her: 'Murderous love. Treacherous love. Deadly love. Love, Love: only living thing in this world. The madness of love.' Elisabeth's cry to George Nelson, although designed to play upon his despair about his sister's death in the convent, is also symbolic of her approach to life at that time:

Save me, Doctor Nelson! And save yourself! No, not with prayers. Not with some righteous abstract alchemy. But with all your body, with all my body. Living flesh of man and woman. ... There's a man to be killed. There is no other way. I am love. I am life. And my need is as imperious and absolute as death itself ... (p 168)

Ironically, this way of life *is* the way of destruction and death. Anne Hébert is no D.H. Lawrence, who looks on the id's sexual energy as a source of joy and creative beneficence. Rather she is one of those modern, gothic writers who 'believe that man carries in his unconscious mind not merely willfulness or the need to indulge himself, but a deep bestiality and dark irrationality.'[3] Although Elisabeth herself chooses 'madness' and passion over boredom, she is always aware of the dark side of the id, aware that violence and cruelty are ready to burst out at any time as 'the underside of all that sweetness.' As she remarks to herself, on viewing Nelson's conspiring with Aurélie, 'You didn't know such villainy was in you, Doctor Nelson. ... All the good topsoil ripped away (pride, self-respect, compassion, charity, courage ...). The heart, stripped bare. So painfully naked. (Fatigue, despair, disgust ...)' To Elisabeth, the murderous and consuming love affair becomes one more sign that 'beyond all saintliness the wily innocence of beasts and madmen reigns supreme.'

As we turn from the younger to the older Elisabeth, it is clear that the superego carries a new psychological weight. The mores and values of society are uppermost in her mind as she desperately tries to preserve the image of respectability provided by her second marriage. As she says,

Jérôme Rolland, my second husband, and honour is restored. Honour. What an ideal to set yourself when love is what you've lost. Honour. A fine obsession to dangle before your nose. The donkey and his carrot. Daily dole at the end of a stick. And the hungry little ass goes trotting all day long. All his life. Until he can't go on anymore. (p 3)

Just as the supremacy of the id resulted in her physical imprisonment, so the supremacy of the superego results in an intangible but equally binding form of imprisonment; she is chained by the values and expectations of her society. Thus the marriage to Jérôme Rolland, which Elisabeth quickly acceded to as a badge of social honour and respectability, comes to be felt as a trap in which both husband and wife are caught. Even as a young girl facing her marriage to Antoine Tassy, she feels 'as if I'm about to drown,' and after the nuptials exclaims, 'I'm doomed!' Her mother dreads having to explain the mysteries of marriage and death to her daughter, which for her are 'one and the same.'

Significantly, it is at the time of her first marriage that Elisabeth senses a division in herself between her conventional actions or appearance and her instinctive feelings – a conflict between superego and id forces which begins a build-up of psychic tension:

This distance that ought to be comforting me, this sense of detachment. It's worse than all the rest, seeing yourself as someone else. Pretending to be objective. Not feeling that you and the young bride dressed in blue velvet are one and the same. (p 66)

In an image of mechanism repeatedly used in modern gothic and grotesque writing, Elisabeth sees herself as a 'little mechanical doll, clinging to her husband's arm.' Cast later in the role of Madame Rolland, loving wife, she muses about her double life:

It's no great feat to have a double life, Madame Rolland. But to have four such lives, or five, with no one any the wiser. Yes, that would be harder. Like all those pious ladies, mumbling their endless rosaries, with vipers' venom flowing through their veins. (pp 70-1)

The idea of the *doppelgänger* or double is of course not new with twentieth-century fiction, as anyone familiar with *Dr Jekyll and Mr Hyde* knows. Numerous other treatments of the divided mind appear in nineteenth-century fiction, among such varied writers as Poe, Conrad, James, and Dostoyevsky. Nevertheless, the revelation of Elisabeth's growing psychic estrangement, of the widening gulf between her secret desires and the conformist, socially conscious role she tries to assume, is more obviously modern in the kind of psychological detail it provides.

Although Elisabeth Rolland works hard to keep up her image of honour and respectability, the forces of the id cannot be completely subdued. She cannot refrain from summoning up memories of her past romance, memories about fulfilment of desire which rekindle the passion within her. At times she fantasizes about future lovers and looks forward to her release from her marriage to Jérôme Rolland.

Yet just as her earlier disregard for society's values had resulted in legal accusations, so these brief mental lapses from the control of the superego result in torments of guilt which threaten to overwhelm her:

That's what it means to be out of your mind. To let yourself be carried away by a dream. To give it room, let it go wild and thick, until it overruns you. To invent a ghastly fear about some wagon wandering through the town. To imagine the driver ringing your door in the middle of the night. To go on dreaming at the risk of life and limb, as if you were acting out your own death. Just to see if you can. Well, don't delude yourself. Some day reality and its imagined double are going to be one and the same. No difference at all between them. Every premonition true. Every alibi gone flat. Every escape blocked off. Doom will lie clinging to my bones. They will find me guilty, guilty before the world. It's time to break free, break out of the stagnation, now. To stifle the dream before it's too late. Quick, into the sunshine. Shake it off. Throw off the spectres. (p 17)

Interestingly, although Elisabeth has little regard for religion, except as another form of social ritual which she publicly adheres to, she still retains a sense of sin and spiritual guilt, a characteristic typical of contemporary French-Canadian literature. Elisabeth Rolland's narrative makes repeated reference to her soul and to the possibility of damnation. She recalls her aunt's warning as she begins her affair with George Nelson: 'Sometimes you seem to forget your soul, my child,' and her own response: 'It's so easy to forget your soul, Aunt Adelaide.' A kind of female Faust, she plunges deliberately along her chosen path, even though she knows it is the path of damnation. 'My soul will have to take strange paths to catch me,' she says, acknowledging 'a voice, inside me. (It can't be my own, I'm much too happy). Telling me loud and clear: "We're going to hell now, all three of us".' It is no accident that, as she recalls Nelson in the early stages of their affair, she sees him sitting on the ground with his body against a tree, 'as if nailed to a cross.' Moreover, she pictures the horse which carries him on his frenzied, murderous journey to Kamouraska as the 'dark, demonic beauty, like the devil himself.' Although Elisabeth reminds herself that English law assumes they are innocent until proven guilty, she cannot so easily brush away the fear raised by the question of her inner self: 'Is it sin?'

As the novel proceeds, psychic tension between the two sides of Elisabeth's personality builds to a point where mental collapse seems imminent. What Elisabeth Tassy had accepted rather complacently in her earlier days as 'this total, sharp division of being,' begins to threaten the sanity of Madame Rolland. She cannot escape a growing sense of darkness or doom by unconsciously accepting either the demands of the superego or of the id. On the one hand, if she allows the defences of the superego to collapse again, 'madness will rise again, reborn from its ashes. And once again, I'll be its victim, bound hand and foot, by so much kindling for the eternal flames.' Indeed at the end of the novel, the maddening, nightmare forces of the id burst through again, and the guilt it occasions reaches its furious climax with Elisabeth imagining herself alone and ostracized as 'wicked Elisabeth! Damnable woman!' On the other hand, even as she tries to pull herself together, to regain control of her imaginings, she knows she can never escape another kind of doom. The Tassy family machine and the requirements of her society seal her fate; they condemn her to 'the icy mask of innocence. For the rest of her days.' Thus the physical destruction which ends the black romantic tale of Elisabeth Tassy and George Nelson becomes the psychic destruction evident in Elisabeth Rolland's narrative. Against the physical death which concludes the former, there is the death-in-life existence of the older, anguished woman, an existence common to so many modern gothic and grotesque works of fiction.

Despite the religious image of damnation which recurs throughout the novel, there is no clear religious or moral order underlying *Kamouraska*. Rather the novel seems to project the common, contemporary feeling of despair or spiritual meaninglessness. To Elisabeth life is a 'miserable world' full 'of savage mysteries' in which there seems no point. Antoine's violence is a reflection of the fruitless search within himself for 'that unbearable, debasing, degrading something down at the very roots of his being.' Elisabeth knows that Antoine's attitude in turn is but a reflection of George Nelson's own misery; both men share 'a silent, premature experience with despair.' Nelson's concern and compassion for his patients are a desperate attempt to forge some meaning out of life, an attempt which ends in ruin when the saintly healer becomes the demonic destroyer.

The persistent use of animal imagery to describe humans provides a further indication of a savage, meaningless world, 'red in tooth and claw.' Descriptions of humans as animals, although evident from earliest times, have been a repeated characteristic of modern gothic and grotesque writing, as readers familiar with Franz Kafka or Eudora Welty will recognize. In twentieth-century literature, such imagery most often suggests the grotesque, spiritual pointlessness of human existence; man is, to use William Van O'Connor's phrase, 'caught in his own biological nature.'[5] In *Kamouraska*, as Elisabeth's narration begins, she reveals that she is stared at 'like some strange beast.' Her husband, Jérôme, lies defenceless in his bed, like 'an oyster caught without his shell.' To Elisabeth, man is 'one long snake, always the same, coiling himself about in endless rings.' Even God himself is depicted as just another kind of powerful, savage beast ready to pounce; at death, one discovers, 'the hand of God seizes its prey.' The sense of human animalism is most vividly portrayed in the hunting scene. Elisabeth and Antoine stalk each other as they stalk the geese and ducks: 'You're on my trail now, stalking me like a good hunting dog. And I'm getting your scent too and tracking you down.' The story shows that not only is Elisabeth an easy mark for Antoine; he also becomes the hunted prey.

In a world without lasting human values, the animal law of survival of the fittest prevails. *Kamouraska* traces a pattern of predators and victims in which survival is equated with mental rather than physical dominance. Elisabeth survives because of her strong will, and as in many other Canadian gothic works from *Wacousta* onwards, the power of her will is one of the more chilling features of the book. At times the three men in her life seem but a 'triptych' to be manipulated:

I want you to live, and I want him to die! I've chosen you George Nelson, I'm life and death, bound up together for good and all. (p 161)

Even as she becomes the guilt-haunted Madame Rolland, musing over the past, the old sense of power keeps returning:

I have that power. I'm Madame Rolland. I know it all. From the very beginning, I played my part in the lives of these two ill-starred young men. Presiding over their friendship with great delight. (p 121)

Although Elisabeth's will allows her to dominate the people around her, she cannot control as completely the vagaries of her mind and the conflict between the opposing parts of her own psyche. Her heightened psychological tension parallels the unresolved conflict between primitivism and civilized society that we have seen in many of the nineteenth-century gothic romances. Elisabeth survives on a physical level, but psychologically she is clearly the victim also. One of the most affecting features of *Kamouraska*'s gothicism, like that of other modern gothic novels, is its revelation that mental horrors are as terrorizing as any external menace. Although its tale of the young lovers has the physical, violent quality of traditional black romances, the psychological thrust of *Kamouraska*'s outer frame reveals a contemporary attitude – that the dark wilderness of the mind can be haunted by as fearful presences as ever stalked the forests and castles of old.

8

Sociological Gothic:
Wild Geese and *Surfacing*

The term 'sociological gothic' may seem a paradox, since the two components are usually associated with contrasting streams of fiction. While gothic elements belong with the fantastic world of romance, sociological approaches are connected with realistic or analytic fiction. Nevertheless, a sufficient number of twentieth-century Canadian novels seem to present this paradoxical mixture to justify a special category in this analysis of modern gothicism. Martha Ostenso's *Wild Geese*[1] and Margaret Atwood's *Surfacing*[2] provide two examples, separated by nearly fifty years, of the sociological gothic: the first was published in 1925 and the second in 1972.

Wild Geese is part of a substantial body of fiction which portrays life in the prairies and which is often called regional literature. Such fiction is seen to present the attitudes and characteristics of the people of the area with the authority of truth. Yet clearly the truth often moves from accuracy to exaggeration, from the social realism, of, say, John Marlyn's *Under the Ribs of Death*, towards the heightened depiction of life found in some of Frederick Philip Grove's fiction, such as *The Yoke of Life*. *Wild Geese* is an example of the prairie novel which is ostensibly realistic and sociological, but which emerges with demonstrably gothic qualities.

The social realism of the book has often been discussed. In his introduction to the novel, Carlyle King maintains that

Ostenso catches the feeling and flavour of a pioneering farm community, and she pictures with sympathetic understanding the customs and superstitions, the crudities and the kindnesses, of the Icelandic, the Hungarian and other new settlers. She neither magnifies nor denigrates a way of life on the farm that was usual in Western Canada a generation ago but is now largely changed; she does not romanticize, she represents.[3]

Although King's denial of any romantic elements in the book is surprising, certainly many of the descriptions of the actions and attitudes of prairie people are compatible with other non-fictional accounts, and there is a sense of verisimilitude in the portraits of many of the Bjornasson family, the Thorvaldsons, and Mrs Sandbo. The land to which they are intimately tied is seen to shape the quality and conditions of their existence. Mark Jordan, a visitor from outside and thus an observer rather than a settler, comments that 'we are after all only the mirror of our environment.' His long, philosophical speech to Lind Archer analyzing the influence of the land – how its austerity reduces the possibility of outward expression of feeling among the people – is as intrusive in the narrative as a direct lecture from the author. It reflects a belief in environmental conditioning or determinism common among many 'sociological' novelists from John Steinbeck to Theodore Dreiser.

Lind, the visiting school teacher, also comments on the shape of the rural society. It has become a straightjacket of propriety for herself and Mark, whom she can meet only infrequently because she recognizes 'the malicious nature among the settlers. The intolerance of the soil seemed to have crept into their very souls.'

These sociological aspects are countered, however, by a growing gothic element. The mood of the story is one of fear. Lind notices a tension in the family from the moment of her arrival, and gradually becomes aware that the farm is a 'sinister' and 'dread' place. The oppressive silence which characterizes the family meals, like the silence in *Wacousta*, only heightens the sense of impending catastrophe – that 'something dreadful is about to happen.'

The physical environment itself, although bleak and harsh, gradually develops into more than a neutral, natural phenomenon and becomes a darkly gothic force. At best it manifests itself as part of a mysterious universe, indifferent or cold to man's plight, from which he is forever estranged and isolated. The wild geese are a particular symbol of this aspect of existence, and to Lind 'their cries smote upon the heart like the loneliness of the universe.'

Increasingly, the universe shows a malignant rather than an indifferent side, becoming an active rather than passive menace. The land seems to become a cruel tyrant, harsh and demanding. The muskeg especially is representative of this dark, demonic side; it is 'bottomless and foul,' 'black and evil,' and at the end of the story it becomes an actual and symbolic path to Hell for Caleb Gare, as 'the insidious force in the earth drew him in deeper' to his death.

As suggested by the preceding passage, Caleb Gare is an agent as well as victim of this evil. He is first depicted as an ugly giant with 'tremendous shoulders and massive head which loomed forward from the rest of his body like the rough projection of rock from a cliff.' His startling black brows and beady eyes add to the picture of an ogre; it is not surprising that when he smokes his pipe Lind is reminded of 'the fixed sardonic face of a fakir, lifting his eyes upward to catch the demoniacal image of his conjuring.' Gare's appearance is merely a signal of his behaviour, and his behaviour is a reflection of his single-minded obsession with the land.

A related, terrifying aspect of Gare's behaviour is the strong will he exerts over his family, a characteristic frequent in Canadian gothic fiction, as noted earlier. Gare is the tyrant who, like the fool in the sermon, 'eateth his own flesh,' turning his children into grotesque, repressed victims as 'twisted and gnarled and stunted as the bushland he owned.' Over Judith especially he tries to exert his will; since she had a will of her own, 'she would have to be broken.' Although the farm to which he chains them is a prison for all the family, Judith hates it the most and longs to escape.[4]

Gare's wife, Amelia, also submits to the power of his will and to his blackmailing hold upon her. When she went to bed after one of his subtle threats, 'fear beat on her heart like the wings of some ominous bird.' She sees her own life as a kind of grotesque tragicomedy – as if she had been 'dragged terrified out upon a stage to play the leading role in a tragedy at which the audience would laugh.' Her existence is a death-in-life one, and even the land around her she views as 'growth – with death in its wake.'

Although Gare seems an agent of a malevolent physical environment, he still fights for supremacy over it. From the outset he senses that natural forces are stronger than his will. Viewing the physical deterioration of Anton Klovacz, he reflects anxiously, 'Disease – destruction – things that he feared – things out of man's control.' Although he cannot fully control nature, it is clear that Gare will go to any length to impose his will on his family. When Judith's rebelliousness becomes too much for him, and Amelia at last refuses to cower under the whip-hand of his will, he explodes with physical violence and cruelty, tying his daughter up in the barn and beating his wife. Yet in the end the villain is undone. The raging fire, which creates the hell on earth for Gare that he had created for others, spells the end of his demonic rule.

As in *Wacousta* and many other gothic stories of both the nineteenth and twentieth century, a contributing factor in the gothic character of *Wild Geese* is a sense of strong and often strange sexuality. And as in *Wacousta*, Kroetsch's *The Studhorse Man*, and *La Guerre, Yes Sir!*, the relationship between sexuality and violence is close. The centre of this sexuality is decidedly not Mark and Lind but rather Judith. Like Carson McCullers' Amelia in *The Ballad of the Sad Café*, Judith is far from the stereotyped feminine heroine; she has a masculine manner and seemingly bisexual appeal. Like McCullers' Amelia she has a hard-fought wrestling match with her would-be lover. Only after Sven has won the match by bending Judith's arm almost to the breaking point does Judith want him to kiss her.

Although Lind's relation to Mark in the romantic sub-plot is conventionally sentimental, her relationship with Judith, like that between Clara and Madeline de Haldimar in *Wacousta*, has lesbian undertones. Seeing Judith for the first time, she notices her 'great giant body, her chest high and broad as a boy's ... she wore overalls and a heavy sweater, and stood squarely on her feet, as if prepared to take or give a blow,' and when Judith approaches her 'with a heavy swinging stride,' Lind thinks 'she had never before seen such vigorous beauty.'

In a description similar to Hazard LePage's view of Martha Proudfoot in *The Studhorse Man*, Lind at one point sees Judith as akin to a horse, remarking 'how strangely beautiful she was. Like some fabled animal – a centauress perhaps.' The horse has traditionally been an image of animal sexuality, which Judith, like Martha Proudfoot, so obviously possesses. When she forcefully struggles to break in the horse to the point where her wrists bleed, her intention is probably the bridling of sexuality which the saddled animal conventionally represents. It is clear, nevertheless, that the violent ride which Lind watches admiringly is a pleasurable sexual release:

When it was over Jude unsaddled the panting, froth-covered animal and threw herself down beside Lind and Martin.

'Nothing like a little exercise to make you feel good,' she said, wiping her wrists. Her cheeks were deep red and little beads of moisture shone on her tilted upper lip. (p 39)

Considering the violence and sexuality of *Wild Geese*, the mysterious and destructive role of nature, and the wilful evil of Caleb Gare inflicted upon his imprisoned family, one is not surprised that a gothic atmosphere gradually overrides both the elements of social realism and Lind and Mark's sentimental love story. From a fairly restrained, although ominous beginning, the mood of menace and terror moves toward a finale as melodramatically gothic as in many nineteenth-century black romances. In this finale, as in many other of its aspects, from the wilful, obsessive protagonist to the lesbian undertones to the sentimental sub-plot, *Wild Geese* is perhaps the nearest twentieth-century counterpart to *Wacousta*.

By comparison with *Wild Geese, Surfacing* has little sense of melodrama. The sociological element is, however, much more obvious. In many ways, the novel seems a fictional counterpart of Margaret Atwood's *Survival*, a thematic study of Canadian literature which has much to say about Canadian society. Many of the themes it discusses under such headings as 'Animal Victims' and 'Ice Women Versus Earth Mothers' are evident in the novel; and of course the role of victim itself, the pivot of her thesis, plays a part in the story also.

The sociological side of *Surfacing* is complicated by the fact that the story, like *Kamouraska* and unlike *Wild Geese*, is a first-person narrative, and the narrator herself shows increasing psychological strain and mental instability. This makes it more difficult to identify the narrator's reflective passages of sociological comment as the author's views.

Nevertheless from the first page it is apparent that the experiences and perceptions of the narrator have some connection with Canadian society as a whole. Moreover, as with so many Canadian works past and present, the depiction of Canadian life is linked with a view of American life. An early image of death provides a clue to the feeling of anti-Americanism which pervades the story. The birch trees in the area are dying, and it is stated that 'the disease is spreading up from the south.' More direct evidence is given in the opening description of Joe, the narrator's lover, who from the side is

like the buffalo on the US nickel, shaggy and blunt-snouted, with small clenched eyes and the defiant but insane look of a species once dominant, now threatened with extinction. (p 8)

The anti-American feeling becomes even more pointed later in the story, when the narrator has time to mediate on her situation. Accused by her companions of hating men, she replies, 'It wasn't the men I hated, it was the Americans, the human beings, men and women both.' Although these observations are made by the narrator, it is clear that a negative view of Americans is not hers alone. David, the would-be film maker, keeps repeating 'bloody fascist pig yanks' throughout the story, as if the epithets were part of the nationality.

On a sociological level, the term 'American' may be seen as a synecdoche of western technological society. It is the social manifestation of a specific attitude, that is, of an excessive belief in man's rationality and his ability to dominate both his own body (by suppressing natural passion) and the world around him. *Surfacing*, like George Grant's *Technology and Empire*,[5] suggests in the term 'American' a repressive, technological imperialism which is the legacy of a combined liberalism and Calvinism. Canadians have also succumbed to the American influence, as the narrator realizes. When the fishermen turn out to be Canadians rather than despised Americans, she calls them Americans anyway. She realizes that she herself has followed the rationalist attitudes of the Americans just as her father had done, he who constructed a wall of order and reason with which he faced the universe. She muses that

At some point my head must have closed over, pond freezing over a wound, shutting me into my head; since then everything has been glancing off me, it was like being in a vase, or the village where I could see them but not hear them because I couldn't understand what was being said. Bottles distort for the observer too: forms in a jam jar stretched wide, to them watching I must have appeared grotesque. (p 106)

Although the narrator realizes that other people may have seen her previous emphasis on the mind as grotesque, she still does not see herself or the issues with clear-eyed vision; she is not yet free from the distortions of her own subjective and disturbed feelings. Despite her denial of emotions, it is her pent-up, emotional reaction, albeit largely uncommunicated to others, which largely creates the gothic atmosphere in the novel.

Thus the sociological case against Americans becomes consumed in paranoic hatred. The Americans are depicted in her imagination as menacing invaders ready to destroy Canadian victims. The case is not kept impersonal – as 'American attitudes' or 'American way of life' – but personal: the American as human is an enemy. At one point there is even a comparison between the Americans and Hitler, a comparison which, although coolly presented, is symptomatic of the gothic heightening the term 'American' has undergone in the narrator's mind. The narrator suggests that the evil which Hitler embodied did not die with him but 'it was like cutting up a tapeworm, the pieces grew.' The latter image suggests that evil is somehow out of control, an ever-increasing force which cannot be destroyed.

It is possible, of course, to see an ironical approach on the part of Margaret Atwood toward anti-Americanism. That David, whose attitude is the most abusive, is also a fanatic fan of American baseball increases the suspicion of irony. The obvious paranoia of the narrator as she retreats into her lair from the searchers, imagining an American invasion, suggests that her anti-American feelings are symptomatic simply of encroaching madness. However, the ironic approach is hard to credit, when one considers the ending of this story. Even when the narrator conquers her fear and decides to return to society as a partial answer to her problems, she thinks of 'the pervasive menace, the Americans. They exist, they're advancing, they must be dealt with, but possibly they can be watched and predicted and stopped without being copied.'

Although the Americans seem to represent the primary evil in the book, the narrator's response to them is part of a larger anxiety, which while less conscious, is nonetheless pervasive. As in most of the other works discussed, the anxiety here is linked to a sense of being caught between two equally dangerous alternatives, the double menace of nature and civilization. The external conflict may in turn be connected to the internal conflict between primitive emotions and rationality displayed by the narrator.

Although nature in the end is seen as a life-giving force, during the length of the narrator's stay on the island it becomes a threat similar to that facing Susanna Moodie in *Roughing It in the Bush:*

Sometimes I was terrified, I would shine the flashlight ahead of me on the path, I would hear a rustling in the forest and would know it was hunting me, a bear, a wolf or some indefinite thing with no name, that was worse. (p 73)

A state of nature is a state of evil as much as of grace. Obviously, the narrator does not adhere to a Rousseauistic notion of natural innocence. City children, she maintains, are no more cruel than wilderness ones: 'To become like a child again, a barbarian, a vandal: it was in us too, it was innate.'

Civilization is also a threat, even aside from the menace of American technological imperialism. There are suggestions that any society is dangerous or threatening. Not only is it 'unsafe' to live in a city, but those friends from her society who she brings with her are viewed as agents of entrapment. Just as the inhabitants of the island are entrapped by nature, so relationships with each other become prisons. The narrator does not trust anybody, whether Evans, the boat man, or Joe, her lover; everyone is a spy and she his victim. Anna, whom the narrator views with growing distaste, becomes the epitome of modern society to her, an artificial woman whose make-up masks the emptiness and ugliness behind it.

An associated gothic element in *Surfacing*, beyond this sense of double menace, is the awareness of death which, like a grim spectator, keeps intruding upon the story. The death of the narrator's parents, especially the father, whose mysterious disappearance provides the motive for the visit to the island, contributes to this awareness. Equally important factors are the recurring images she sees of violent death and murder. Thus David's needless catch of the fish is referred to as a killing; the narrator is an 'accomplice' in an act of 'murder,' and the fish itself is a 'cadaver.' Similarly the blue heron, senselessly slaughtered, is left to hang as proof of man's 'power to kill.' Later the narrator sees herself as a murderer who through an abortion destroyed life within her. Even Joe is viewed as an agent of violence; rather than creating art, he mangles his pots, 'mutilates, cutting holes in them, strangling them, slashing them open.'

The terror of death for the narrator lies partly in its mysterious incomprehensibility. Unlike the deaths in Anna's detective stories, the death she sees all around her and the capacity for murder within all humans are lacking in explanation. Unlike her brother, she is not a 'realist about death,' and the illogical images of dead and murdered beings keep returning like ghosts to haunt her. At the same time she finds herself becoming increasingly deadened.

Towards the end of the story, the narrator's distrust of society and the destructive rationalism it represents precipitates her total withdrawal. She escapes into a lair and tries to reach the spirit of her parents by becoming a part of the natural world. The new appreciation of her mother, of mother earth itself, and of the creative 'id' side of her own nature are interrelated. Yet her attempt to rejoin body to head is not without its own difficulties. At one point the sense of new life within her seems to be achieved at the expense of the death of all reason; insanity threatens the new state of bliss. Thus the completely natural woman is 'killed' to avoid the new danger of ending up in 'the hospital or the zoo.'

In the end the narrator seems to recover her mind as well as her body, and to take a new, more hopeful attitude towards the society and the civilization she has rejected. She perceives that the American advance must be halted; Joe and the people in the city are not yet Americans. Canadian society, like the individuals who comprise it, is only half formed and therefore still able to be shaped. While she still hates the Americans, she refuses to be a victim and tentatively returns to Joe and to civilization. Yet even here dangers await. Something Anna stated earlier points to these dangers: 'when the heartline and headline are one you are either a criminal, an idiot or a saint.' The narrator knows the dangers of this tentative rapport with civilization, but she also knows the alternative – death for herself and for her society.

It is apparent by now that there are considerable differences between the sociological gothic aspects of *Wild Geese* and *Surfacing*. Margaret Atwood's novel is altogether more didactic and prescriptive in its representation of society than Martha Ostenso's, as well as better written. In *Wild Geese* reasons are given for existing conditions of prairie society, but there is little consideration as to how it might be changed. *Surfacing* is also more continuously analytic. While the social message is perhaps most obvious at the beginning and end, there are throughout the story indirect social comments linked with the narrator's perceptions and attitudes and with those of her companions.

Although there are passages of social comment interspersed in *Wild Geese*, the gothic mood of fear, present even in the first chapter, gradually overwhelms the realistic or sociological aspects of the book. The story moves towards a melodramatically gothic climax, undiluted by the sentimental love union which forms a minor postscript to the drama. In *Surfacing*, by contrast, there is little melodrama from beginning to end; even in the animal-like retreat to the lair, the narrator's introspective reflection about herself and its implication for society are emphasized more than the bizarre actions she takes.

Yet despite their differences, both books provide evidence that the unlikely or seemingly paradoxical mixture of sociology and gothicism is a recurring combination in twentieth-century Canadian fiction. They illustrate that, despite the interest in social realism or social analysis in many modern novels, the gothic spirit hovers close by the fictional scene, frequently throwing dark shadows over the landscape and its inhabitants.

9

Terrible Grotesque:
Mad Shadows

Mad Shadows is the earliest and blackest product of Marie-Claire Blais's fiction.[1] The gothic atmosphere of menace, of something dreadful awaiting round the corner, is apparent from the initial chapter, with its disclosure of Isobelle-Marie's festering unhappiness and jealousy. The sense of impending doom is realized when three out of four of the main characters meet an early death.

The terrors of death and dying, observable in almost all gothic works, are thus a major aspect of the sense of menace in *Mad Shadows*, and the fear of aging which dominates two of the characters is a variation on the theme. Moreover, throughout the book the sense of bodily disfigurement or disintegration is a recurring spectre,[2] to the point where Lanz actually seems to decompose before he dies. The menace of evil, that other central theme of gothicism, is also constantly present and at times, ironically, death seems the only hope of escape from it.

Following in the traditional pattern established by 'Monk' Lewis and others of the *Schauer-Romantik* stream, Blais creates gruesome images which build to a crescendo of horror. For example, Patrice is implicitly compared to a vampire when it is stated that 'he sucked their [the family's] blood ... in order to rest,' or in the description of his flaccid face with 'the lips of a corpse.' In a similar gothic vein, Isobelle-Marie's black dresses are described as clinging like 'a shroud' and her face when she confronts her mother is 'glowing with blood and saliva.' Louise's cancerous growth on her cheek is a 'sinister tendril' which resembled a 'tear of blood,' and later it 'blazed with an even more lurid glow.'

As well as retracing conventional, gothic patterns, *Mad Shadows* also fits the grotesque mode. Although we have seen that the gothic and the grotesque are frequently used as interchangeable terms,[3] there are certain features especially associated with the latter term, and one of these is its emphasis on physical deformity. Although Kayser rightly asserts that physical ugliness is not synonymous with the grotesque,[4] physical deformity is, as Lawson states, 'the one characteristic of grotesque literature that all critics stress.' It plays a strong part in grotesque literature as in grotesque art and sculpture; the monstrous misshapen bodies and faces found in painting from Bosch and Bruegel to Goya and Hogarth have their counterpart in writings ancient and modern, be it Chaucer's repellent Pardoner and Summoner or McCullers' cross-eyed giantess of *The Ballad of the Sad Café*.

The protagonist of Marie-Claire Blais's grotesque novel is an ugly, emaciated girl, with a body 'as mean as a dented sword.' Nor is Isobelle-Marie the only deformed or ugly person in the story, since she marries a blind boy and gives birth to a daughter who like herself 'belongs to the race of ugly.' Her stepfather, Lanz, is crippled. Her idiot brother Patrice becomes grossly disfigured with a scalded, scarred face. The beauty of her mother, Louise, is destroyed by a cancerous growth on her face which 'clawed its way along the flesh.'

All this ugliness in *Mad Shadows* obviously is not a naturalistic slice of life in some sordid backwoods corner of Quebec. As critics have often stated, the locale in the story, like that in *Le Chercheur de trésors*, seems to exist by itself, apart from any realistic context of time or place. Unlike the grotesque visions of Sherwood Anderson or Erskine Caldwell, or even some of Blais's later works, the grotesque here has a broadly spiritual or metaphysical rather than social context. It deals with universal rather than particular cultural problems.

Indeed *Mad Shadows* seems so far removed from the light of common day as to resemble a dream state. The grotesque, like the gothic, has often been associated with the sinister dream, from the time of the early sixteenth-century synonym for the grotesque – 'sogni dei pittori' (dreams of painters)[6] – to the more recent writing of Poe and Kafka. The poetic quality of Blais's prose, the flattened two-dimensional nature of the characters, and the absence of realistic detail contribute to the dream-like atmosphere. Moreover, the relatively bare recitation of the narrative action, with little of the speculation or topical digression which creates a more relaxed atmosphere, suggests the ungovernable, driven quality of a dreadful nightmare.

Much of the physical deformity and ugliness is symbolic of a spiritual deformity; the characters' mean and diseased bodies reflect souls that are monstrous. However, unlike the grotesque characters in Chaucer's pilgrimage, in which each ugly, physical feature is an outward and visible sign of an inward, invisible disgrace,[7] in *Mad Shadows* there is no established moral order or standard of perfection to which the deviations or deformities can be symbolically tied. *Mad Shadows* is therefore a disruptive rather than directed grotesque work. The physical ugliness and widespread deformity is a sign of a general collapse of values, of a world in which there is no heaven but a hell of human unhappiness and depravity. The story traces the descent of Isobelle-Marie and those around her to their individual infernos; the fire which destroys the farm at the end of the book with 'a vast apocalyptic roar' is an actual and symbolic finale to their agony of suffering, loneliness, destructiveness, and hatred – to a 'disintegrating world' where only evil seems to flourish.

The grotesque element in *Mad Shadows* relates to an abyss in which traditional values, beliefs, and hopes have fallen.[8] God no longer seems to exist in the world of the characters. The sense of a disintegrated or a lost Christian tradition is strongly felt in the grotesque distortion of traditional Christian symbols. The symbolic bread and wine of the sacrament of the eucharist, with its message of sacrifice, love, and spiritual sustenance becomes distorted into a sadistic rite as Isobelle-Marie systematically starves her brother of his customary meals of bread and wine during her mother's absence. Later in the story, she sits down with her newly engaged mother to a dinner which is supposedly a celebration but is actually an ingestion of hatred and despair.

The rite of baptism is ironically distorted when Isobelle-Marie plunges the head of the unsuspecting Patrice into boiling water; the Christian symbol of spiritual grace and purification becomes perverted to a symbol of empty destruction and self-centredness. A distorted replay of the Genesis drama is suggested in the remark that 'such temptation must have possessed Eve as she prepared to seduce Adam.' The story continually plays upon the image of water as a deathly rather than redemptive force. When Patrice escaped from his beating by Lanz, he was 'like a man who has been saved from drowning but who still battles the ocean within himself,' and the ocean within is a bloody one.

The suffering by water which Patrice undergoes is matched by the ordeal by fire which consumes Louise and the farm. Yet there is no rite of purification associated with the flames. The final fire is obviously both a symbol of earthly apocalypse and a glimpse of the spiritual hell to which the characters had been descending throughout the book.

The loss of God experienced by the characters is not to be construed as a complete indifference to God. Their spiritual agony, inarticulated and often unrealized, is indicated by their search for a replacement as a centre of meaning. The ugliness which seems to overcome all the characters is not only symbolic of their spiritual corruption but of a false substitute for God sought in beauty. Thus the *process* of physical deterioration is an important element in the drama of the book. Beauty becomes a false god for Louise as she vainly tries to preserve her own fading beauty. In her warped attitude ugliness is, if not the equivalent of evil, at least a source of distaste and horror. She at first refuses to recognize the growing blemish on her cheek and then desperately tries to mask it with make-up rather than accept the need for bandaging. She loves the beauty of Patrice, seeing in him a reflection of her own beauty and consequently of her self-worth; Isobelle-

Marie realizes that Louise's 'whole being rested on this solitary and fragile beauty.' When her son's face is burned, Louise cruelly withdraws from him just as she had been repelled by Isobelle-Marie's ugliness.

In this context it is Louise's obsession with beauty more than her growing ugliness which makes a grotesque of her. In her grotesque illusion about beauty she is similar to the grotesques described by Sherwood Anderson in *Winesburg, Ohio:*

It was the truths that made the people grotesque. The old man had quite an elaborate theory concerning the matter. It was his notion that the moment cne of the people took one of the truths to himself, called it his truth, and tried to live his life by it, he became a grotesque and the truth he embraced became a falsehood.[9]

Where Anderson suggests that all absolute values are deforming, Blais concentrates on one false absolute.

For Lanz, appearance is all that matters also. He 'whose gods were his clothes, his women, Louise's jewels and a gold cane,' knows no other role to play in life than that of a man of fashion. Isobelle-Marie thinks of the approaching wedding of Lanz and Louise as the marriage of a 'pair of dolls,' artificially pretty and empty of feeling or understanding. The image of dolls is repeated constantly with reference to both Louise and Lanz. It is a variation of the human mechanism image mentioned in the discussion of *Wacousta* and frequently found in grotesque writing – a ludicrous version of the common gothic motif of obsession. Thus Louise is referred to as a 'frivolous doll' or 'pretty doll,' who never suspected that one day 'she would lie battered and abandoned'; Lanz has 'the graceful, congealed laughter of marionnettes.'

Patrice, the 'Beautiful Beast,' has a face and body that are close to physical perfection. Despite his idiocy, he gradually becomes aware of his own beauty, aided by his mother, who 'introduced him to vanity by placing him in front of mirrors.' Like Narcissus, Patrice likes to contemplate his appearance reflected in the lake, until one day he discovers the connection between his beauty and his happiness: 'From then on beauty was to become the goal of his life. Patrice had become the god of Patrice. His soul was too feeble to ask for more.' Just as physical beauty is experienced as sensual pleasure by all the characters, so beautiful Patrice is primarily a sensuous character. Every physical stimulus makes him shiver, and like the cats in the woods with whom he senses his kinship, he is driven by the instinctive urges of his body. He craves the sensuous excess of violence and wild horseback rides.

Naturally when Patrice's face becomes disfigured by fire his happiness is gone. No longer worshipped by his mother, he sinks to depths of neglect and despair.

Fear grips him when he glimpses the reflection of himself in the lake; the ugliness of his body becomes 'the prison of his fear' from which he cannot escape.

Isobelle-Marie's desire for beauty is no different from the others, despite an intelligence and understanding which is much greater. Acutely conscious of her own ugliness and the exclusion from her mother's attention it causes, she is uncontrollably jealous of her brother's beauty and wreaks her revenge upon it. Perceiving that her one chance of happiness lies in becoming beautiful, she pretends to the blind boy that she is. Thus Isobelle-Marie and Michael are united in their ideals as much as in their bodies for, as Blais remarks, 'in them burned a longing for perfect beauty.' The false cycle begins – pretended beauty leads to expressions of love, which in turn transforms Isobelle-Marie's ugliness into an odd kind of beauty. She discards her black clothes for white ones as the juices of new life surge within her. Yet just as the actual beauty of Louise is destined to be lost, so the pretended beauty of Isobelle-Marie is even more fragile, gone with the first glimmering of her husband's restored vision. Michael beats her and leaves her on account of the ugly reality.

Even before this tragic reversal, it appears that Isobelle-Marie's status as a beauty is not enough for her to overcome her own distaste for ugliness. Despite a certain intermittent affection for her daughter, Anne, she is horrified and repelled by her hideous features. When Michael scorns Isobelle-Marie, she also withdraws her tender feelings towards the child, often wishing she would die.

If beauty in *Mad Shadows* is an illusory god, love offers no salvation either. Unlike the solution to human difficulties offered by love in some of Blais's later writing, in *Mad Shadows* love is only a short-lived phenomenon or an illusion. The love of Louise for Patrice, Lanz for Louise, and Michael for Isobelle-Marie is based only on physical attraction and cannot survive. Interestingly Blais suggests the possibility of a love which is 'pure' – that is, without sexuality – in the early love of Isobelle-Marie for Michael, a love not yet shattered by the onrush of adult passion and 'the wounds of the flesh.' Isobelle-Marie realizes that she and Michael have to end their happy, childish games and to become like Louise and Lanz, part of 'a vast tragedy in which they were all brave performers.' In the undercurrent of horror attached to full sexuality Blais seems to follow in the Jansenist tradition, despite her vehement condemnation of such an attitude in the portrait of the grandmother in *A Season in the Life of Emmanuel*. She remarks that Louise and Lanz 'spent whole days and nights together in a savage exchange of bodies, as tho' offering flesh to be eaten; they were vile, unwholesome.' Violence and cruelty seem in Blais to be an inseparable part of the sexual union. She neatly juxtaposes in the same short chapter Michael's brutal and selfish killing of the butterfly and Isobelle-Marie's announcement that she is pregnant.

Much of what passes for love in *Mad Shadows* is really self-love. Louise loves

Patrice inasmuch as his beauty reflects upon herself, and Patrice of course is in love with his own image. Lanz's self-centred love attempts to smother Louise's maternal instincts 'in order to take complete possession of his wife, even though it might make her suffer.' Isobelle-Marie's alternately tender and cruel treatment of her brother reveals her selfishness; she realizes that part of her desire to hurt her brother is her masochistic fear that she will lose him.

The theme of self-love is prevalent in modern American gothic fiction, as Irving Malin has pointed out.[10] The characters in the fiction of Carson McCullers, Flannery O'Connor, and Eudora Welty, for example, are obsessed with themselves; they cannot enter the social world except to dominate their neighbours. Blais's characters also compulsively follow Narcissus. The more they love themselves the less they can escape their private world; their isolation grows. Michael is a symbolic extreme of the pattern. In his blindness he is entrapped in his own world; he 'constructs the world within himself.'

In *Mad Shadows*, the mirror serves a complicated function. For many characters it is an altar of perverted self-love. Patrice kneels in adulation before his own reflection in the lake and spends much of his time at home alone in front of his mirror. After his disfigurement and subsequent confusion, he wonders why his image has become so ugly, and unknowingly asks a question of considerable metaphysical significance in the book: 'Am I a mirror or am I Patrice?' Burdened with terror at the sight of himself, he had 'lived so long with mirrors, in front of mirrors, inside mirrors. All his memories were superimposed as in a nightmare.'

Louise also spends her time in front of mirrors and it is not surprising that in the final days of her life, when the cancer has wasted her away, Isobelle-Marie finds her, still kneeling before her own image. Her ultimate isolation from God and her attempt to create a God in her own beauty are suggested in her final dying plea, when she prays to God in heaven but 'her mirror did not answer.' Significantly, in the finale to the story, Patrice returns to the ruins of her house to discover that it is 'a world of ashes and broken mirrors.' Unable to find his beautiful face in the lake, he plunges after it and is lost, the victim of an illusion, but one who has at last broken through the reflection of himself which imprisoned him.

Clearly, as well as being an altar of self-worship, the mirror is a trap of subjectivity. In *Mad Shadows* there are no objective values; reality is seen through a mirror in which the self is the only constant, crowding the scene. Characters are cut off from each other's understanding and are isolated and fearful. Patrice, who lacks the common human bond of reason, is the most completely entrapped in the prison of his fear, unable even to understand what is the matter with himself let alone his relations to others. The conventional gothic motif of imprisonment – for example, the actual physical imprisonment in *Wacousta* and *The Golden Dog*, or the symbolic, cultural imprisonment in *Wacousta* and *Le Chercheur de trésors* – seems to become in *Mad Shadows* a kind of philosophical entrapment, the separation or estrangement of the self from any reality or meaning outside it.

Although this subjective imprisonment of the characters, and the inadequacy of love and beauty as keys to escape, leave a bleak picture, the terrifying aspect of Blais's grotesque vision goes beyond a sense of philosophic meaninglessness. It relates to a malignant, destructive force seemingly threatening from the void. Episode after episode in the novel asserts the strength, and at times the primacy, of evil. The scene with the mad inmate called Faust underlines the seemingly inevitable pact with the devil which humans make during their confinement in this insane world.

Blais's vision of a disintegrating, sinister existence has a religious focus. She does not attribute the cruel viciousness and grotesque nature of people to their grotesque milieu, as does Erskine Caldwell, or see man absurdly 'caught in his own biological nature,'[11] as does William Van O'Connor, but points to strangled, withered, or unrealized souls. In *Mad Shadows* original sin seems a fundamental precept. Although Isobelle-Marie's deliberate viciousness is partially the result of maternal neglect and harshness, a harshness which she in turn adopts with her own daughter, Michael's cruelty to spider and butterfly while in the happy prime of his youthful love is wanton and unprovoked.

Blais's constant reference to her characters as being either without souls or with deformed souls indicates her preoccupation with spiritual loss. She remarks that Lanz and Louise 'have no souls,' and as Lanz meets his death, the question is raised, 'how could such an empty being die? Lanz felt himself growing cold, he who had never felt of death, nor of the death of the spirit.' After his disfigurement, Patrice no longer means anything to Louise, 'for her soul was that of a doll.' In the course of the embittered exchange between Isobelle-Marie and her mother, 'their souls emerged, grotesque and monstrous.' When we last see Isobelle-Marie, she is leaving the farm which she has burned down, with her mother entrapped in it. What matters at this point is not what will happen to her in society, but her spiritual state:

Weeping she felt the need for a god, one god. The train was coming. She pushed Anne away from her and walked toward the tracks, her heartless soul throbbing with the fear. (p 122)

Unlike the others, Patrice does not have a deformed soul but one which was never formed. His idiocy leaves the spirit within him 'feeble, timorous, overawed – and profoundly empty.' Nevertheless, in a vague, uncomprehensive way he searches for a soul he cannot find. The face he sees in the mirror fills him with pleasure and then with terror, but still he does not know who or what he is; he feels 'like someone being strangled but who still survives within himself.' The question is asked, 'Would a soul finally be reborn within him, like inspiration in a budding genius?' Blais's answer is 'No'; she denies earthly hope to him as she does to all the others, explaining that he has 'the soul of an Adonis but Adonis has been murdered.' Patrice ends a soulless existence by taking his own life. As the author sardonically remarks, in 'the blue of the sky which came after the blue of the water, the Beautiful Beast found his soul at last.'

The repeated mention of the characters' spiritual state and the description of Isobelle-Marie's father as one close to God might suggest a religious agrarianism underpinning Blais's vision. In the latter instance, especially, there is evidence of that traditional association of godliness with a life close to the land. When Isobelle-Marie ravages the farm, she realizes that 'it was God's land she had destroyed.' Similarly, when Isobelle-Marie's father 'tilled the virgin loins of the earth, he was penetrating to the heart of God.' The sexual imagery of the latter reference suggests the goodness of nature itself, an implication reinforced by a reference to the forest as a 'green chalice.'

Nevertheless, the main thrust of the story dampens any such speculation about a philosophic or religious centre found in nature, and on the contrary seems to indicate one more disruptive upending of traditional French-Canadian values. Isobelle-Marie's toil on the farmland can hardly be seen as ennobling or redemptive; it is a defensive retreat into drudgery from the cruelties of her family life, a direction which she quickly abandons when Michael provides a joyful alternative. Moreover, the idyllic time spent by the lovers romping in the woods does not prevent Michael from his cruelty to the insects or from his later violence towards his wife. The actions of the beautiful beast himself hardly suggest spontaneous goodness of one of nature's 'innocents.'

That religious faith in any traditional sense offers an escape from the holocaust of life on earth seems an untenable interpretation in view of the total lack of grace operative in Blais's vision of existence, a point which Naïm Kattan discusses in his introduction to the novel.[12] Life turns sour for all the characters, and misery strikes the undeserving even more than the deserving. Isobelle-Marie's desperate attempt to transform her life through love is cruelly short-changed. The 'miracle' she seeks – that love can create a kind of beauty overriding her natural ugliness – turns to ashes.

Mad Shadows is an example of the disruptive grotesque, since there is no philosophical framework or set of values as an implied norm against which the distortions can be measured or as an escape from the pervasive horror of life. But to say that it is disruptive is not to suggest that it is without meaning, or that it reveals a simple authorial delight in the perversity or depravity revealed. *Mad Shadows* is therefore different from the sensational stream of gothic writing exemplified by some of the early *Schauer-Romantik* fiction or by contemporary popular variations on the Frankenstein theme, in which authors have often seemed to revel in sordid, gruesome details. If Blais attempts to shock with her story, she is not deploying sensation for its own sake. Her attitude seems similar to that espoused by Flannery O'Connor in a quotation from Wyndham Lewis: 'If I write about Hell that is rotting, it is because I despise rot.'[13] Blais's exaggerations or distortions reflect a serious desire to shock complacent readers into a recognition of modern life's horrors. As O'Connor states it, 'to the hard-of-hearing you shout, and for the almost blind you draw large and startling figures.'[14] Her grotesque version of the common gothic themes of sin and death are presented with no playfulness but with a grim, moral seriousness. *Mad Shadows* fits into the pattern of terrible grotesque writing described by Ruskin:

It is not a manufactured terribleness, whose author, when he had finished it, knew not if it would terrify anyone else or not; but it is the terribleness taken from life; a spectre which the workman indeed saw and which as it appalled him, will appal us also.[15]

For Ruskin as for many later critics, the noble quality of the terrible grotesque is its endeavour to grasp the higher spiritual truths of life with a power and insight which brings it close to the sublime:

No Divine terror will ever be found in the work of a man who wastes a colossal strength in elaborate toys; the first lesson which that terror is sent to teach us is the value of the human soul and the shortness of moral time.[16]

If the grotesque magnification of evil is a religious act,[17] then Marie-Claire Blais's grotesque magnification of evil is a religious act without a religion. What we find in *Mad Shadows* is the attempt to see beneath the surface of a seemingly smug world, stripped of the tacit security of rationalization or sociological explanations – an attempt to confront the mysterious and sinister perversities of human existence. Although Blais's constant reference to the symbols and terms of the old disintegrated religious order reveals her groping for some belief, she never finds a new order in this novel. The universe she presents is evil and inscrutable; the only certainty she offers is the continuing, monstrous, spiritual deformity of its human inhabitants.

Sportive Grotesque:
La Guerre, Yes Sir!

In the middle of *La Guerre, Yes Sir!*[1] the young nun Esmalda returns to her home in the village to pay homage to her dead brother, the soldier Corriveau. Obeying her religious order's strictures against entering the house, she views the mourners around the coffin through an opened window and asks: 'Who is dead? Who is alive? Perhaps the dead man is alive. Perhaps the living are dead.' Despite the unthinking, almost mechanical quality of her speaking, the question is important, underlining the complex and problematic issue of death in the novel. In *La Guerre, Yes Sir!* the coffin sits in the centre of the house as it remains in the centre of the characters' consciousness, and it is the symbolic focus of the story's meaning.

Roch Carrier has referred to his writing as 'a funny adventure,' and we can readily see the humour in his first novel.[2] Varieties of humour can be found in almost every section, from the farcical fairness of Amelie's every-other-night policy with her two husbands, to the sexual jokes unconsciously contained in the prayers of the villagers, to the satirical bite in the depiction of Bérubé's first sexual encounter and in the priest's eulogy. Using Ruskin's terminology, it can be said that the novel moves away from the terrible towards the sportive grotesque. In other words, in Carrier's grotesqueness play or jest is more dominant than, for example, in Marie-Claire Blais's grotesque writing.

However, it is also clear that fearfulness is always present in the playing and that Carrier's mockery carries with it an almost constant undercurrent of horror. The bizarre and amusing actions of the characters have much in common with the type of black comedy found in *Le Chercheur de trésors*, a novel which Carrier admits he was much influenced by and whose motifs he obviously borrowed from. Moreover, as in so many other gothic and grotesque works, in *La Guerre, Yes Sir!* images of death are a primary source of the fearful or horrifying aspect.

The sense of death on a personal, physical level is of primary concern to the characters, a reality brought home to them by the returned body of one of their own villagers. He is treated as a hero, although we learn that he has been inglori-ously killed in action while relieving himself behind a hedge in the army camp. Mother Corriveau questions the purpose of a life which leads inevitably to the grave:

What was the use of having been a child with blue eyes, of having learned about life, its names, its colours, its laws, painfully as though it was against nature. What was the use of having been a child so unlucky in life ... Everything was as useless as tears. (p 94)

Where Mother Corriveau weeps in response to death, her husband Anthyme rages; where she attempts prayer, he can only swear.

The menacing fact of individual physical death is a metaphor for other kinds of death and dying which spread in widening circles of implication through the story. The unconscious blasphemies of the mourners' prayers emphasize the spiri-tually moribund condition of a people for whom their religious teaching is ironic-ally itself a kind of death force. The priest tells his parishioners that life is unim-portant except as a prelude to death and final judgment, 'that we live to die and we die to live.' His Jansenist sermon portrays a vengeful God, and warns of the torments of Hell awaiting mankind with its 'Sinful, voluptuous nature,' and es-pecially awaiting those people who stray from the prescribed devotions. The nar-row emptiness of his message is a bitter satire upon the whole Church, with its glorification of war and admonition to overburdened women to produce more children – the latter a grotesque and deadening distortion of the life force. The nun mouths the platitude, 'How sweet it is to come back among one's own peo-ple,' while remaining apart in the cold outdoors. The decayed teeth in her wan, thin face suggest that submission to the Church's dictates results in a withering of humanity.[3]

The characters in *La Guerre, Yes Sir!* also face a cultural death; their sense of identity as individuals and as a community is being increasingly repressed. The villagers are powerless against the authority and force of the English-speaking soldiers, and in the end are thrown out of their own house by these strangers. The uncomprehending sergeant disdainfully views the 'pigs' who do not even speak a civilized language, and whose behaviour throughout the night is proof of the truth of his old history lesson on French-Canadian animality. Bérubé, who attempts to bridge both French and English cultures, is caught in the middle. At the conclu-sion he faces the prospect of his dismal future; considered by both sides to be a traitor, he is condemned to be a perpetual outsider. Thus the novel repeats the pattern of fear found in *Wacousta* and *For My Country* in which the notion of cul-tural annihilation is a primary anxiety; it reinforces the idea that collective social menace as much as individual menace is a recurring motif in Canadian gothic fiction. Yet there is a difference between Tardivel's nineteenth-century, French-Canadian version and Carrier's contemporary novel. In *For My Country*, the enemy is clearly defined as the non-Catholic, notably the Freemason and English-Canadian Protestant, while the French-Canadian ideological fortress of religion and *patrie* is still intact. In *La Guerre, Yes Sir!*, by contrast, the garrison has all but fallen, having been undermined from within as well as from without.

The enemy is also more nebulous, wearing many faces besides that of the *maudit anglais*. Despite the dominance of the soldiers and the subsequent resentment of them by the villagers, the awareness of menacing, cultural annihilation is more than the threat of English masters overriding French-Canadian victims. Margaret Atwood takes too limited a view of the menace in her analysis of *La Guerre, Yes Sir!*,[4] when she emphasizes the two opposing cultures. The threat is also a matter of modern technological society stamping out indigenous cultural mores and desires, of massive, impersonal forces acting against the villagers' feebler human particularities and peculiarities. As the railway station employee observes, 'It's a war of the big guys against the little ones. Corriveau's dead. The little guys are dying. The big guys last forever.'

There is a gradually surfacing fear that even the big guys are on a path to destruction, that humanity as a whole will march to a mechanical doom. In Henri's nightmare, Corriveau's coffin enlarges and all the people in the world march into it 'just as they entered Church, bent over, submissive.' Significantly, the last to disappear are the armies of soldiers, as 'mechanically disciplined' as the group around Corriveau's bier. The latter stand like automatons, rigid and impassive, and even the girls notice 'it wasn't human for them to stay fixed there all night, stiff and motionless. It's not a position for the living.' Thus there is a warning that technological society with its will to power will not only turn man into a desensitized, impersonal robot, but will eventually draw him, ordered and submissive, to his doom. The train, roaring through the snowy wastes into the little village with its mechanized soldiers, is a technological engine of death not unlike the train which intrudes into the woods in Faulkner's 'The Bear.'

The horror of technological society, with its reduction of the spontaneously human to the automatic, is one more version of the gothic-grotesque motif of mechanism first discussed in the analysis of *Wacousta*. Carrier's soldiers, who seem to function without feeling and to move without motive, other than obedience to orders or the fulfilment of a mindless drill, represent the ultimate in dehumanization. In this, as in other modern grotesque works, technological automation suggests something demonic beyond the logical implications of a powerful system. It invokes fear of a world which is actively menacing as well as incomprehensible. In Henri's nightmare, the soldiers are like mechanical toys drawn by a central control in a little box, which marches them back into its depths and shuts the lid on them.

Despite the importance of death as a symbolic focus, Carrier's novel is not simply a tale about death, but as Nancy Bailey points out, it presents a battle between life and death[5] in which the two forces are often surprisingly confused. This confusion and the resulting sense of both death-in-life and life-in-death is a key to much of the grotesqueness in the book. The nun's question reveals her uncertainty as to who is really alive, despite the Church's teaching that life after death is the only valid life. Henri senses that life on earth has become a living death, that 'man is unhappy wherever he is,' but like the other villagers, he fears the truth of an afterlife in which the flames of Hell and purgatory torment all sinners.

Despite the forces of death which threaten to squash their humanity, the villagers have an irrepressible desire for life:

The villagers were alive, they were praying to remind themselves, to remember that they were not with Corriveau, that their life was not over; and all the time thinking they were praying for Corriveau's salvation, it was their own joy in being alive that they proclaimed in their sad prayers. (p 48)

Corriveau underlines their life-in-death desire when he complains that if life must 'stop at a coffin, it was not fair for people to have an obvious love of life.'

Many of the activities of the villagers are a mixture of life and death forces. Although the eating and drinking bouts lead to a brawling, destructive conclusion, they are in themselves a defiant display of sensuousness. Mother Corriveau's cooking becomes an almost savage attack on death in which she sweatily beats at the pie dough, sensing that the perfume of the golden, baked tortière is the essence of living; she explains that 'when there is a dead man in the house, the house shouldn't smell of death.' In this role she becomes a kind of earth mother, a characterization which Carrier explores more fully in the second novel of the trilogy, *Floralie, Where are You?*.

Sex is both an instrument of death and of life. On the one hand, the Germans are described as killing women by raping them, and, to the sleeping Molly, the attacks of her loveless husband cause dreams of a knife tearing her stomach open. On the other hand Molly, a prostitute, represents the happiness of living to all the young soldiers who used to come to her. For Bérubé, the initial thought of sex outside a Church-blessed marriage leads to visions of damnation; yet with Molly in bed with him as his wife, 'it was death that they stabbed at violently.'

The pervasive violence also represents a confusion of life and death forces. In the story we find father beating up son, husband against wife, neighbour against neighbour, English against French, and the omnipresent spectre of the world war itself. The war beyond the village acts only as a catalyst for the war within. The violence is an expression of the villagers' intellectual and spiritual isolation from each other, of the decline of commonly held cultural values and the resultant profound ignorance and misunderstanding of each other. The violence is destructive, but it is also a positive response to repression. It is a sign 'of vitality badly used,'[6] of an upsurge of life in a society where there is no common language of meaning but body language.

The recurring images of blood and snow suggest the dual implications of violence. At various points in the book, blood spills on the winter snow, whether it is the blood of the amputated hand or the beaten-up faces of the villagers in their battles with each other and with the soldiers. Snow is a traditional image of purity and innocence. In French-Canadian literature, it is also an image of isolation and the inward-looking naïveté or sterility it produces. Maria Chapdelaine comes to mind, as do the words of the familiar song by Gilles Vignault: 'Mon pays, ce n'est pas un pays, c'est l'hiver.' The French-Canadian garrison is built of snow and ice as much as it is reinforced by religious and nationalist principles. The bloody brawls are obviously disfiguring, cruel, and destructive. At the same time the blood that spills on the snow as well as on Molly's virginal, white wedding dress may suggest a human sensuous response which overrides traditional 'bloodless' ideals. Carrier's concluding statement in the novel – 'the war had dirtied the snow' – has ironic rather than tragic overtones.

Whether violent or not, many of the activities and actions in the story relate to a selfhood not fully realized, and to a society where it is increasingly difficult to feel at home. At the beginning of the book Arthur tries to persuade Henri to accept the war and his soldier's role as a defence of traditional social values: 'Soldiers have a duty to protect farmers who are fathers of families, and the children and the cattle of the country.' Yet increasingly, Henri realizes his true position: 'his wife no longer belonged to him, nor his animals, nor even his children.' The characters' bizarre actions reflect their estrangement, their inarticulated anxieties about an alienated life.

Sherwood Anderson has related the quality of grotesqueness in people to a single-minded pursuit of partial truths.[7] Ronald Sutherland has also suggested that Carrier's characters are grotesques because they cling to outworn truths.[8] Thus Mother Corriveau's desperate observance of religious practices becomes grotesque in its distortion, and Bérubé's reflex-life response to the values implicit in the soldiers' way of life makes a grotesque of him, as when we see his frenzied and inhuman attempt to make a good soldier of Arsène. At the same time the characters may reflect D. W. Robertson's definition that the grotesque 'is a monster because of unresolved conflicts in his makeup'[9]; sometimes 'the grotesque pretends to be one thing but is actually something else,'[10] as is the case with Esmalda in particular. The unresolved conflicts often have to do with spiritual values or social attitudes which the character has ostensibly accepted, and another reality which he actually practises. The source of humour as well as of fearful meaninglessness or absurdity partially comes from his divided response.

In a more formal way, the grotesque quality of Carrier's writing relates to a constant juxtaposition of extreme incongruities. Repeatedly he combines the extreme poles of the sacred and profane in Quebec life, a characteristic similar to that found in the late gothic phase of medieval art, and which Charles Muscatine associates with a loss of purposeful direction in the culture.

Its religion is incongruously stretched between new ecstasies of mysticism and a profane, almost tactile familiarity with sacred matters. Its sense of fact is often spiritless or actually morbid. For all its boisterous play, the age is profoundly pessimistic; it is preoccupied with irretrievable passage of time, with disorder, sickness, decay and death.[11]

In *La Guerre, Yes Sir!* we find that the twin 'spiritual' values of patriotism and religion are incongruously yoked with the mundane practicalities of everyday living: the flag is a table cloth; the image of Christ on the cross merges with that of a stuffed pig; Mother Corriveau's prayer becomes an unconscious blasphemy when her Hail Mary invokes a picture of the pregnant Virgin. Similarly in Mireille's dream her toes become transformed into waxen votive candles. Sometimes the grotesque incongruity is achieved by yoking something tragic or horrible with something comical. Thus Joseph's amputation of his own hand to avoid going to war is horrifying, but it becomes grotesque when the hand is casually substituted for the frozen turd and used as a hockey puck, that commonplace of Canadian life. Disruption or confusion of our usual single response (the comic laugh with the tragic cry and the gothic gasp) reinforces our awareness of the confusion of the traditional world views and values.

There is a literary resonance in this latter image of the amputated hand which Carrier seems to be playing upon. As Madame Joseph snatches the hand from the child and tucks it under her coat before going on her way, one immediately recalls that other grotesque occasion in *Le Chercheur de trésors* when Charles Amand snatches the *main-de-gloire* from under the noses of the medical students. The act of dismemberment is yet another variation on that recurring motif of bodily disfiguration in French-Canadian literature. Joseph's self-mutilation may be seen as a parody of the motif by a kind of *reductio ad absurdum*; Carrier may also be extending the gothic death motif by a symbolic suggestion of cultural masochism or suicide.

In other ways *La Guerre, Yes Sir!* plays with or disturbs our literary expectancies, further providing a sense of strangeness or estrangement. The view from the window in which a captive being (usually a woman) looks out from her 'prison' is a repeated motif in gothic literature, but also has a special place in Quebec literature, where the captive spirit often symbolically represents the isolated containment of French-Canadian society, cut off from participation in the larger outside world. One remembers Elisabeth Rolland in *Kamouraska*, and the image of Maria Chapdelaine looking out both longingly and in fear upon the forest and its avenues of escape, from the confinement of her backwoods house. In the opening scene of *La Guerre, Yes Sir!* Joseph found, after cutting off his hand, that 'the cloudy window separating him from life gradually became very clear, transparent.' He had a brief moment of lucidity, in contrast to the image of Isobelle-Marie in *Mad Shadows'* opening scene, where she presses her face against the train window but soon sees nothing outside it. In nearly all cases there is a sense of a claustrophobic confinement behind the window. In *La Guerre, Yes Sir!*, it is a nun standing outside in the cold who is cut off and who is left to gaze through an open window at the bustle of activity within. In this image Carrier does not seem to imply a reversal of customary meaning, that is, he does not seem to suggest that the inner group rather than the outer world is the source of vitality. After all, there is death inside the room as well as without, in the coffin as well as in the decayed teeth of the nun. The nun's puzzling question as to who is alive and who is dead would rather suggest that Carrier means simply to disrupt or disturb the customary image and its cluster of associations.

Taken as a whole, the effect of *La Guerre, Yes Sir!*'s striking images is to startle the reader's thoughtful response rather than direct it; despite the visual clarity and dramatic impact, the images are most often ambiguous and paradoxical in their symbolic implications, unlike Carrier's later *Floralie, Where are You?*, in which the allegorical push is stronger and more insistent. Thus in this first novel in the trilogy, the grotesque alliance of horror and humour is essentially disruptive. Yet despite the sense of estrangement or absurdity which the disruptive grotesque usually expresses, *La Guerre, Yes Sir!* does not project a vision of annihilation but of cultural alteration.

Critics such as Ronald Sutherland have been quick to point out the similarity between Faulkner's *As I Lay Dying* and *La Guerre, Yes Sir!*.[12] Both stories revolve around a coffin, and describe the grotesque behaviour and attitudes of rural characters in response to the death of one of their own. The American's novels, like Carrier's, reflect what he regards as the moral confusion and social decay of his society, and, as Malcolm Cowley remarks, Faulkner is 'continually seeking in them for violent images to convey his sense of outrage.'[13] Faulkner's characters, like Carrier's, have a double meaning besides their place in the story, also serving as symbols or metaphors with a general application. In both novels, the incidents in the story represent forces and elements in society, although neither *As I Lay Dying* nor *La Guerre, Yes Sir!* can be explained as a connected, totally logical, allegory.

However, I think there is a fundamental difference in emphasis between *As I Lay Dying* and *La Guerre, Yes Sir!*. In the former novel, the smell of putrefaction, both literal and symbolic, hangs heavier in the air. Although some of the characters occasionally show signs of Faulkner's later statement that 'man will not merely endure; he will prevail,'[14] survival seems an individual achievement in the face of a general social decay. In *La Guerre, Yes Sir!*, by comparison, the collective assertion of life is as pronounced as the smell of Mother Corriveau's cooking. What one senses in the grotesque distortions and inversions of dying values is the presence of change as much as of destruction; it is less a story of death than of metamorphosis. The general sense of confusion – in the characters' attitudes, in the symbolic values which issue from the story, and in the response of the reader – are signals of this process. Old shapes and images shift; patterns dissolve and the disparate elements come together in startling new associations.

Carrier's reference to his trilogy as a depiction of 'the Middle Ages of Quebec' reinforces this notion of change rather than doom as his central theme. In Carrier's reference, the Middle Ages stretches from a period before the Second World War to the middle sixties, and encompasses the end of the parochial period, the discovery of the outer industrial world and the passage from country to city life. The medieval analogy is apt, since the twentieth-century decades in Quebec, like those of earlier times, present an inward looking, church-dominated world, in which the old ways are no longer life-giving forces. It marks a time in which the gap between ideal and real, seen by many critics as the essence of late medieval 'decadent' gothicism, becomes an abyss in which the traditional beliefs and social values are to tumble. Yet society did not collapse at the end of the Middle Ages, but was infused with a new life; the Renaissance was a transformation of the old into new modes of activity and awareness.

In *La Guerre, Yes Sir!* the Renaissance is not yet accomplished, but the process of change has begun. The novel is disruptively grotesque, not because of any overriding feeling of futility, but because there is no specific moral or philosophic framework against which the grotesque distortions may be judged. Carrier gives no real hint of the shape of things to come, but the undying energy of his characters and the constant upsurge of humour against horror, precludes a vision of total despair. In *La Guerre, Yes Sir!*, as in the later *Floralie, Where are You?*, the process of metamorphosis is one in which the old grotesque encasements of society must be broken through, or overturned and discarded, before a new, freer being will emerge. In this sense, then, the wooden box carrying the body of

Corriveau and by implication the whole of Quebec society is less a coffin than a cocoon.

To point out the element of optimism underlying Carrier's vision is not to undercut the emphasis on fear or horror. The individual characters themselves obviously live in a world of increasing uncertainty or absurdity, and it is clear that a man like Bérubé faces a personally meaningless and menacing future. Nor can the resurgent humour and playfulness in Carrier's depiction of French-Canadian society be considered frivolous. In discussing the sportive grotesque, Ruskin distinguishes between its noble and ignoble forms:

For the master of the noble grotesque knows the depth of all at which he seems to mock, and would feel it at another time, or feels it in a certain undercurrent of thought even while he jests with it; but the workman of the ignoble grotesque can feel and understand nothing, and mocks at all things with the laughter of the idiot and the cretin. [15]

La Guerre, Yes Sir! both mocks and distorts in its depiction of French-Canadian life, but the disruptive vision of confusion and change does not reflect a light-headed abandon. Rather Carrier fills Ruskin's prescription of thoughtful feeling; his sportive grotesque alliance of humour and horror is the play of a serious mind.

11

Symbolic Grotesque:
The Double Hook

To describe Sheila Watson's *The Double Hook* as 'symbolic grotesque' may seem odd, since it is evident that most if not all grotesque literature has a symbolic element.[1] The reason for so describing it lies in the greater emphasis on symbolism in this variety of grotesque, an emphasis which is linked with the directed nature of most symbolic grotesque works. In the symbolic grotesque, the symbols tend to be explicit or conventional and to fit fairly neatly into the underlying moral or philosophic framework; they are an integral part of the story's message or direction. In disruptive grotesque fiction by comparison, where there is no such direction or underlying purpose, the symbols frequently have a diffused or diverse suggestiveness, with a tangential rather than integral relationship to each other. They tend to enrich and broaden the meaning of the work but are not necessary to a basic understanding of it.

In *The Double Hook*, the symbolism clearly has a central, directive role, and when it is combined with Watson's careful, measured use of words, the effect is similar to those modern gothic novels described by John Aldridge as 'pure, neat and carefully refined as symbolist poems.'[2] Yet unlike many symbolist poems, this modern gothic novel offers an obvious moral or philosophic position underlying the story.

The message of *The Double Hook* is religious. It is a story about redemption written from a Christian vantage point. In this respect as in several others, it resembles the fiction of Flannery O'Connor, who is also concerned with redemption and writes within a Christian symbolic framework. O'Connor maintains that the Christian writer has the sharpest eye for the grotesque; he will find in modern life

distortions which are repugnant to him, and his problem will be to make these appear as distortion to an audience which is used to seeing them as natural, and he may well be forced to take even more violent means to get his vision across to this hostile audience.[3]

Watson's grotesque novel would seem to follow O'Connor's reasoning, but whereas *The Double Hook* shows salvation within reach at the ending, Flannery O'Connor's stories usually finish with defeat and destruction, only indirectly pointing to the path of Christian redemption through the abysmal effects of evil, anti-Christian behaviour and attitudes.

Despite the optimism of *The Double Hook*'s ending, at its centre there is as bleak a picture of existence as ever painted by Flannery O'Connor. The short tale contains repeated scenes of violence, cruelty, and victimization – traditional evils of gothic fiction. James murders his mother and seduces Lenchen; Lenchen becomes pregnant and is abandoned by James and her mother; Greta commits suicide by setting fire to her house; James blinds Kip.

Moreover despite the absence of the gross physical abnormality or monstrosity found in Flannery O'Connor's fiction as well as in that of Marie-Claire Blais – there are no cripples, amputees, or hideously deformed individuals – the characters are nonetheless grotesques. Part of this grotesqueness is attributable to the one-dimensional quality of their portraits. In none of the characters do we get much complexity in response or attitude. The only picture we get of Mrs Potter is of an old woman ferociously fishing, and the widow Wagner is reduced to a cardboard figure who repeats 'dear God' over and over. Such single-sidedness or single-mindedness is of course one of the marks of human grotesqueness in literature, as Sherwood Anderson has pointed out,[4] but in *The Double Hook* it reaches the point where it is easy to interpret the various characters as representatives of certain types. Although there are no strictly allegorical figures boldly labelled Greed, Sloth, and so forth, the characters are flattened, and certain symbolic qualities are stressed. In his introduction to the story, John Grube states that Mrs Potter is a symbol of death and William is the man of 'reason, order and commonsense.' Similarly, Felix represents spiritual awakening through love, and Kip is a symbol of amoral instinct or innocent perception.

Although Coyote plays a more complex role than many of the characters, he can be seen as a variation of the conventional Faustian figure. Leslie Monkman has discussed at length Coyote's position as a trickster, an immoral source of seduction and death who functions in satanic opposition to the Old Testament Jehovah.[5] Until the end, Coyote is not seen by the inhabitants, who only hear his call or mark his footprints, and it is this sense of mystery surrounding him which raises the fear in the people to gothic proportions. Cleverly utilizing the terror he arouses, Coyote seductively lures Greta with the charms of death and tempts the widow with forgetfulness. Both Mrs Potter and Kip become agents of his dark ways.

The landscape in *The Double Hook* is as grotesque as the characters. The parched, cracked land in which creeks and grass have dried up, cattle are stunted, and dust is everywhere seems monstrously deformed and ugly. The drought is a major cause of the hardship and suffering of the characters, forcing their awareness of the cruel mysteries of life. The landscape, however, is also symbolic; it is a spiritual wasteland which reflects the inner sterility of the characters.

The symbolism which Sheila Watson uses in creating this spiritual landscape is guided by her Christian perceptions and conviction, as various critics have pointed out.[6] Following the story's familiar pattern of spiritual death and rebirth, and of regeneration through love, many of the natural features have dual, symbolic functions, representing both the unregenerated and regenerated sides of existence. The natural world as a whole has a double side. On the one hand, it is menacing and cruel, as when Ara sees the sky like a 'raw skin ... drawn over them like a sack.' When Lenchen seeks refuge at Felix's house, 'in the sky above evil had gathered strength.' The rain which falls at the beginning of the book is 'like a web,' and it has the effect of beating upon the characters 'with adder tongues. With lariats. With bullwhips.' When Ara envisages Mrs Potter fishing, she sees the rising creek as death:

As she watched the old lady, Ara felt death leaking through from the centre of the earth. Death rising to the knee. Death rising to the loin. (p 21)

On the other hand, when the characters' lives become regenerated, nature increasingly reflects the change. Previous images of sterility and death are counterbalanced by the traditional, Christian image of water as symbolic of spiritual rebirth. The clearest image of redemptive nature occurs when James returns home to begin afresh with his people; he goes through 'a meadow of wild hay, watered by some hidden spring.' Correspondence between the internal and external state is emphasized with the description of the widow as she decides to find her daughter, 'her face stirring like ground cracked above a growing shoot.'

The recurrent play upon fish and fishing also illustrates Sheila Watson's deliberate use of a single symbol for multiple effects, as opposed to two contrasting symbols. The fish is, of course, a conventional symbol of Christ. Mrs Potter is repeatedly seen by the other characters, fishing in the dried-up stream, but her catch, unlike Christ's, never feeds the multitude of her neighbours. Rather, Mrs Potter in her fishing is a kind of death symbol and anti-Christ, who 'throws her line' against God and against any loving relationship with her family. Both she and James, by attempting to 'fish for glory,' catch fear and darkness on their hooks. Moreover, as Grube points out, the 'kettle of fish' prepared by the prostitute in the brothel is rejected by James as a kind of false hope. It is symbolically fitting that before he sees his way to any redemptive role, Felix stands meditating with a fish spine in his hand. The regenerative implications of the fish symbol are evident in the final chapter, as Ara prophetically sees a 'great multitude of fishes.' Significantly it is 'St Felix' who catches a fish in a stream and shares it. The reversal of James's previous role and that of his mother is suggested during his return to the settlement, when 'fear unwound itself again like the line from his mother's reel.'

Although the underlying Christian framework is a major factor in the symbolic directedness of the story, there are clearly other levels of suggestiveness which have no Christian reference. The symbolic figure of Coyote is from American Indian myth and, as Grube mentions, Sheila Watson uses a symbolic pattern of the elements – fire, earth, air, and water – that are basic to the 'collective unconscious' of the human race, to 'the racial memory of man.' One also finds conventional cowboy story symbols in the story. In the cowboy story use of a stark, desert setting, the stereotyped black-and-white characterizations, and the ideas of justice, revenge, and outlaws, *The Double Hook* provides a North American variation of the wasteland story. In its directedness, the cowboy story may also be considered a North American rendition of the old morality play.

Nevertheless, it is also possible to interpret the cowboy features as a disruptive rather than directed grotesque element. Sheila Watson herself refers to the story as an 'anti-Western,' a comment which suggests her parodying purpose. She may be attempting to explode the clichés she exploits by emphasizing the dehumanized, crabbed lives of people who live like literary caricatures – a converse of the earlier interpretation in which characters follow literary convention to direct us towards their mythic or universal human qualities.

Whichever way one chooses to interpret the cowboy motifs, it is evident that in her use of conventional religious symbols Sheila Watson provides a deliberate duality which underscores her view of the unavoidable duality of existence. Kip's comment about James, used as the epigraph to the story, stresses a central theme of *The Double Hook:*

He doesn't know you can't catch the glory on a hook and hold on to it. That when you fish for the glory you catch the darkness too. That if you hook twice the glory you hook twice the fear. (p 61)

This theme underlies gothic fiction in general, which attempts to shock the reader into a recognition of the dark or evil side of life which people try to ignore or explain away. The universe which *The Double Hook* presents is dark with cruelty and inexplicable suffering. Sheila Watson demonstrates that the habitual reactions of the members of the settlement aggravate and expand their misery and make grotesque their lives.

On the one side there are those who react passively. Such passivity can be seen as an aspect of the dominant Calvinist ethos, which stresses the insignificance of man and his work beside an omnipotent and stern God, and sees salvation bestowed upon the chosen few rather than earned by right actions. Thus the attitude to God is mostly one of helpless fear, as the widow Wagner indicates:

Dear God, she cried. Then she stopped short.
Afraid that he might come.
　　Father of the fatherless. Judge of widows.
Death and after death the judgment. (p 55)

Fear of death is entangled with fear of God's harsh justice after death: 'Dear God, she thought. How easy death would be if there was death and nothing more.'
　　This passive fear of death and darkness leads to the death-in-life existence which is characteristic of much gothic and grotesque fiction. The habitual posture of waiting for something terrible to happen contributes to the atmosphere of tense expectancy and of nameless menace which is characteristic of the book. Before Mrs Potter's death, all her family had lived 'suspended in silence' and inaction:

They'd lived waiting. Waiting to come together at the same lake as dogs creep out of the night to the same fire. Moving their lips when they moved them at all as hunters talk smelling the deer. Edged close wiping plates and forks while the old lady sat in her corner. Moved their lips saying: she'll live forever. And when they'd raise their eyes their mother was watching as a deer watches. (p 43)

The whole world seems hung in passive apprehensiveness. The boy notices that 'All about him as he rode into the yard he could hear the breathing of his animals. Close to the house waiting.' And the widow despairs: 'The country. The wilderness. Nothing. Nothing but old women waiting.' At times the passive response to suffering makes death itself seem a desirable escape, an escape which Coyote offers. Coyote calls to James, 'in my fear is peace,' and the boy also hears his beckoning cry, 'in my mouth is forgetting/in my darkness is rest.'
　　The deadening encroachment of fear upon those who respond passively shows itself in a repression of all human warmth and sympathy. Angel has been married to Felix for several years and borne his children, but Felix knows they lived together 'by necessity. By indifference.' Theophil, to whom Angel turns, wants even less real involvement with her.

All the time, he thought, people go shutting their doors. Tying things up. Fencing them in. Shutting out what they never rightly know. (p 58)

Fear of human attachment is mixed with fear of sexuality. The widow rejects Lenchen when she can't face the shame of her daughter's pregnancy. Greta, who turns everyone away from her house, can stand only the embrace of Coyote's seductive death call:

And Coyote cried in the hills;
I've taken her where she stood
My hand is on her head, my right hand embraces her. (p 85)

Angel realizes that she lives in a community of 'empty spaces.' Later she discovers there is no escape from such isolation by moving elsewhere: 'But if loneliness is being in one's own skin and flesh, there's only more lonely beings there than here.' An adjunct to the repression of emotion is the preference shown by some of the characters for ignorance rather than knowledge or vision, since such knowledge or vision might demand action or involvement in the community. Thus Theophil 'lets fear grow like fur on his eyes,' and tells Kip 'sometimes, too, it's better for the eyes to close.'

Although the characters' passive response to their suffering contributes to a more fearful, repressed, and lonely existence, some of those people who respond actively also bring darkness and destruction upon themselves and others. Mrs Potter chooses actively to defy God and to assert herself in God's place:

If God had come into the valley, come holding out the long finger of salvation, moaning in the darkness, thundering down the gap at the lakehead, skimming across the water, drying up the blue signature like blotting paper, asking where, asking why, defying an answer, she would have thrown her line against the rebuke. (p 20)

Because she is more strong-willed than the others, Mrs Potter is able to dominate her family. Her will turns the passive compliance of her son and daughter into seething frustration. She brings destruction upon herself and her children; she is the cause and recipient of her son's murderous explosion and the indirect cause of her daughter's insane self-destruction. Mrs Potter's dominance continues after her death. People report that they see her; she remains in their minds despite her physical absence. She still influences her children's actions. Greta tries to assert her will as her mother had done before her, and James, after his one act of defiance against his mother, returns to his fearful defensiveness and distrust of others. In his desire for self-importance, he also 'fishes for the glory,' copying the very attitude of his mother that he hated.

Kip is another one who reacts actively, who reaches out for God-like 'white glory' through a controlling knowledge of the weaknesses and strengths of those around him. Like Mrs Potter, he becomes an agent of Coyote's darkness, as the boy Heinrich notices: 'Get out of here, the boy said. Wherever you are there's trouble.' Ironically, despite Kip's perception about others' foolishness, he foolishly goads James into blinding him.

In the end Coyote himself is fooled, since out of the destruction comes signs of a new life built on help and love for each other. Felix and the widow come to the aid of Lenchen, and Felix and Angel renew and revitalize their marriage. James returns to the place and to the people he had tried vainly to forget; in his resolve he finds escape from his despair. However, Sheila Watson suggests not that the power of darkness is eliminated, but that it is recognized and faced with new honesty and determination. The difficulties and the inexplicable suffering are still there, and man will still need a straight back 'to carry round what the world will load on his shoulders.' Moreover, even though the families of Felix, the widow, and James have come to terms with Coyote and his temptations, the downward slope into despair and destruction is yet a danger for the new baby and for all those who set their feet 'on the sloping shoulders of the world.' Although fear is conquered, darkness remains.

Despite the precariousness of the settlement's achievement, the communal feeling at the end points toward redemption. In this final optimism, *The Double Hook* resembles the medieval morality play's spirit more than it does many modern grotesque works, where pessimism and anguished despair seem to pervade. The symbolic nature of the grotesque in *The Double Hook* also brings it close to medieval drama. Obviously Sheila Watson's novel does not have the same degree of direction as those early models. Her symbolism, as we have seen, contains a deliberate double-sidedness and is sometimes more suggestive than specific. Nevertheless the symbolic structure of the story places *The Double Hook* within a conventional Christian context, in which redemption is made possible through love and charity to one's neighbour. Such familiar directioning to the story has a real danger of seeming trite or artificial to the modern mind. *The Double Hook* avoids this pitfall, retaining a literary freshness through the grotesque originality and the spare, elemental style with which the story is presented. Sheila Watson only points the reader toward the regenerated land of her traditional religious vision after leading him through some uniquely haunting territory.

12

Satiric Grotesque:
Cocksure

While the relationship between satire and the grotesque is acknowledged by most critics, there is no unanimity about the terms of this relationship. Is the connection between the two necessary or merely a matter of frequent association? Wolfgang Kayser states that satire is related to caricature, which in turn 'has much in common with the grotesque and may even pave the way for it.'[1] Although he provides many examples of the grotesque appearing in the midst of satiric contexts, his discussion seems confused. In his statement above and in a later reference to 'satire-turning-grotesque,'[2] he implies that satire moves *towards* the grotesque, but at another point he says that one of the basic types of grotesque is the 'radically "satiric" grotesque with its play of masks.'[3] Such seeming confusion is again evident in his discussion of one of the major trends of nineteenth-century art which, he says, 'reaches the grotesque by way of satiric, caricatural, and cynical distortions, that is by way of the comically grotesque.'[4] His statement seems to make a distinction between the comically grotesque features of satire and fully grotesque art. Kayser's apparent distinction is no doubt related to his insistence upon the essential absurdity of the grotesque, upon his view that it is not, unlike most satire, a vehicle of moral reform or philosophical meaning. Such a definition of the grotesque is inadequate to our discussion, which considers the directed grotesque to be one of the two basic categories of grotesque literature.

Northrop Frye's analysis of literary forms is more helpful here in its clarity. He indicates that the grotesque is a necessary element in all satire, asserting that 'satire demands at least a token fantasy, a content which the reader recognizes as grotesque.'[5] Moreover since satire involves an object of attack, it also demands 'at least an implicit moral standard, the latter being essential in a militant attitude to experience.'[6] Thus Frye not only affirms the connection between satire and the grotesque, but provides tacit acknowledgement of the moral directedness of the satiric grotesque.

Mordecai Richler's novel, *Cocksure*, illustrates this satiric double focus on grotesque fantasy and morality.[7] In attempting analysis, one can usefully distinguish between the two levels of satire in the novel – the first a gentle, humorous level dealing with the foibles of man, and the second a more biting, shocking level which attacks gross evils.[8] These two levels in turn involve two different types of the grotesque.

The first level of satire involves the people and activities which touch Mortimer Griffin in his daily life as husband and father and in his part-time position as public lecturer. Griffin himself fits into the common role of *ingénue* evident in many satirical works from Swift to Evelyn Waugh. According to David Worcester, modern *ingénues* have particular characteristics:

They are grey, subdued observers in a world of startling events and startling people. Mild and passive, they are carried along by life's current – sucked into whirlpools, dizzied in rapids, dropped in backwaters. Things happen to them; in so unequal a contest what is the use of making an effort?[9]

Mortimer Griffin does indeed drift through life, but if his educated brain allows him some superior moments of perception, his neurotic personality makes something of a grotesque of him. Griffin worries constantly about himself and about the impression he creates on others. This exaggerated self-concern is ridiculous in itself, as when he agonizes over the racist implications of picking up or not picking up the glove of the coloured girl standing ahead of him in line. Gradually his fears and anxieties become obsessive, a condition which we have seen to be typical of much grotesque fiction. The culmination of neurotic worry about his sexual adequacy is his sexual impotence.

Griffin's follies are sometimes an extension of prevailing social attitudes, which Richler satirizes by means of grotesque exaggeration. Yet Griffin is more often the passive victim of others' foolishness than he is the butt of his own. Often Richler treats him with the same gentle irony with which Leacock treats Dean Drone – half sympathetic and half reproving – rather than applying his sharp, satiric knife. The other characters which are a part of Griffin's domestic or personal life are drawn with a more dispassionate, unsympathetic eye. On this level of folly, Richler creates characters which, on the one hand, are familiar enough to be recognizable types and, on the other hand, are exaggerated enough for the satire to be effective.

This method is best appreciated by distinguishing between the different varieties of satiric portrait or caricature which various critics have in part or in total seen as grotesque. As early as the eighteenth century, Cristof Martin Wieland distinguished between: true caricature, 'where the painter reproduces natural distortions as he finds them'; 'exaggerated caricature, where, for one reason or another, he enhances the monstrosity of the subject without destroying its similarity to the model'; 'purely fantastic caricatures, or grotesques in the proper sense, where the painter, disregarding verisimilitude, gives rein to an unchecked fancy.'[10]

Most of the 'foolish' characters in *Cocksure* fall into the second category. Joyce Griffin is an exaggeration of a recognizable type of faddish woman striving to stay 'with it' in a rapidly changing world and ardently supporting every fashionable attitude. Her use of clichés ill matched to the occasion is one of Richler's frequent satiric devices, as when she describes the appeal of Ziggy Spicehandler: 'I'd say it's that he has the face of a man who has visited the darker regions of Hell and come back again.'

Miss Ryerson is an exaggeration of the old-fashioned Ontario WASP school teacher, attempting to perpetuate the ideals of yester-year's empire in a decidedly different sort of England from that of her literary dreams. Her hearty clasp of duty ('England needs me') and her confident invocation of traditional solutions against the encroachments of modern cultural and educational laxness are absurd in their inappropriateness. A slightly different satiric technique is used in the characterization of Ziggy Spicehandler and of Jacob Shalinsky, for here the effect is not only related to exaggeration or inappropriateness, but also to an ironic inversion of the familiar or expected situation. Just as Shalinsky, who aggressively barbs and hounds Griffin, is the obverse of the usual persecuted Jew, taunted by a member of the WASP majority, so the racy, coarse Spicehandler, who has assiduously removed all traces of his upper-class origins as Gerald Spencer, reverses the usual trend.

One might wonder at this point why the attitudes and antics of such a group of people should be called grotesque, since exaggeration, incongruity, inappropriateness, and inversion are also familiar comic devices. Certainly the dividing line in satire between what is comedy or burlesque and what is grotesque is sometimes a fine one, and it is possible, as Frye indicates, to see all forms of comic exaggeration as grotesque. However, in this study, as has been previously discussed, the grotesque is considered to combine in varying proportions humour with horror, and it is this latter ingredient which makes *Cocksure* decidedly grotesque in most of its satire.

When dealing with follies, admittedly Richler's satire often begins as pure fun or burlesque, as, for example, the description of Ziggy's film or the early scenes with Miss Ryerson. As the story proceeds, however, a sense of something strange, bizarre, or shocking intrudes – milder terms perhaps than the word 'horror' implies, but nonetheless producing a reaction other than laughter. When Joyce begins to trot out her Freudian jargon to give her son an explanation for his pleasure in a bath, the satire seems straight burlesque, but when her conversations are connected to Doug's frightening nightmares, her continued misapplied psychology becomes grotesque. Similarly Shalinsky reaches grotesque proportions when his single-track obsession with Jewishness prevents him from understanding Griffin and his dire message, that is, when his attitude can no longer be considered harmless. Miss Ryerson's determination to reinstil old academic standards becomes grotesque when she goes to the bizarre extreme of rewarding schoolboy achievement with sexual favours. Nevertheless as long as the character's antics remain follies, the satire which exposes them is decidedly more humorous than horrifying.

The opposite is true in the second level of satire, which exposes characters and actions Richler obviously regarded as evil – a category centring upon the Starmaker and his cohorts. The Starmaker is as truly a gothic creation as Frankenstein, and his plans to perpetuate himself by taking new body parts from people around him and to ensure the popular success of his biographies by killing the subjects are sinister in the extreme. The repulsive ugliness of this man, who prides himself on acquiring a double set of sex organs, makes him the only character in the book who is visually grotesque. It is interesting that when Richler wishes to emphasize genuine malevolence, his portraits move from the second to the third type of grotesque caricature mentioned earlier. The foolish characters, although they are extravagant and ludicrous, still have some affinity with a recognizable model. The Starmaker, by contrast, belongs to the realm of pure fantasy; he is an extreme, macabre creation.

It is as a possibility rather than a probability that the Starmaker is the source of the greatest terror in the book. He goes beyond the distortion of a human trait or attitude, and comes to represent the evil of all superhuman and yet inhuman manipulative forces in the modern world. George Woodcock suggests that the Starmaker is really a figure of nightmare, 'the monster lurching out of dreams and demanding to be clothed in modern guise who inhabits almost every Richler novel.'[11] Like so many gothic villains in Canadian fiction, the Starmaker combines great power with an unshakable will; when he fastens upon Griffin we know the poor man's doom is sealed.

Although the grotesque which Richler creates in *Cocksure* underlines both follies and evils, the moral or philosophic position from which his satiric arrows take wing is less obvious. With satire, the author's stance is revealed often by implicit contrast with the distortions he projects. Yet critics such as Warren Tallman maintain that Richler is simply an iconoclast, skeptical of change and of many of the so-called benefits of modern life; as a writer he is 'cleaning away the debris that has accumulated in a world where all disguises have been put to doubt.'[12] If this were the case, then *Cocksure* would scarcely qualify as directed grotesque fiction, but rather it would be disruptive. Mortimer Griffin would then fit the pattern of modern ironic hero who 'serves no ulterior purpose and reveals no creative thought.'[13] He would be a modern *ingénue* of the sort described by Worcester, one 'who gives off no overtones.'[14]

Richler himself says that 'any serious writer is a moralist and only incidentally an entertainer.'[15] He also maintains that with the breakdown of absolute values in the world, new personal values are needed: 'What I am looking for are the values with which in this time a man can live with honour'[16] – a statement which points to the directedness of his grotesque fiction. In Neil Compton's opinion, Richler is a moral conservative, whose 'black and savage humour stems from a thoroughly traditional sense of outrage.'[17] If we look at Richler's satire, it is evident that progressive ideas, from the Beatrice Webb style of education to sexual permissiveness, are repeated targets, and it might seem reasonable to infer from this choice of targets a conservative or traditional viewpoint. The evil of the Star-maker's biological triumphs similarly suggests a warning about technologically progressive society.

Taken as a whole, Richler's position seems to be more directed than a vague distrust of change or dislike of progressivism. Rather, as Woodcock suggests, he seems to provide a warning against all forms of contemporary collectivity, be it intolerant social pressure, faddish cultural coercion, or corporate impersonality. Joyce is held in thrall to the rule of modish 'in-group' attitudes, just as Shalinsky's preoccupations with the racial group rather than the individual contributes to Griffin's disaster. When anti-puritanism, for which Ziggy is a spokesman, becomes militant and coercive, it creates a different kind of repression, a harmful new puritanism, as Griffin's impotence illustrates.

Perhaps a further clue to Richler's position in *Cocksure* is contained in Griffin's saddened description of himself:

Yes, yes, Mortimer thought, a good credit risk, that's me. Loyal. Hardworking. Honest. Liberal. The well-dressed fellow on the bench in Zoo's story. The virtues I was raised to believe in have become pernicious. Contemporary writing, he thought, is clawing at my balls, making me repugnant to myself. An eyesore. (p 84)

Mortimer sees himself as ugly and grotesque, but ironically, to the reader he is clearly the least grotesque character in the book. His relative normality, as compared to the gross distortions of the other characters, indicates that he embodies what Richler sees as a fundamental decency against the world's conformist indecencies. Griffin's feeble attempts at self-honesty and humanity are inadequate and frequently ridiculous, but Richler directs his satire against his sense of inadequacy more than against his values. Richler has remarked that

The ideological origins of *Cocksure* were to invert in a sense the fumbling Jewish hero of contemporary fiction, and to see how far one could make a case for that easily or glibly dismissed, middle-class, decent, bill-paying, honorable man.[18]

Griffin's deportment has its own folly, but his downfall is largely linked to his susceptibility to the follies and evils of other people. Although the attitudes and values which Griffin expresses are neither the whole lesson of the story nor representative of its entire body of philosophic thought, clearly Richler has provided a moral centre to his grotesque satire in that 'much abused man, the square.'[19]

13

Towards the Mystical Grotesque:
Beautiful Losers

The affinity between the grotesque and mysticism is easily understood. Critics such as John Ruskin and William Van O'Connor maintain that the writer of the grotesque, like the mystic, is seeking the sublime, but that he seeks it in seemingly perverse ways. O'Connor states, moreover, that for modern writers the grotesque 'is the closest we can come to the sublime.'[1] Flannery O'Connor's fiction illustrates this point. Although there is a mystical use of Christian symbols, the emphasis is on the grotesque. The grotesque obliquely points to the sublime by exaggerating the obverse.

Leonard Cohen's *Beautiful Losers* also seems an attempt to express mystical vision utilizing the grotesque mode.[2] As such it is an example of directed grotesque fiction. At the same time, Cohen's mystical attempt fails, and the result seems, in part at least, inadvertently grotesque. The complication of this initial assessment reflects what is undoubtedly a complicated novel; in interpreting it one confronts many difficulties and uncertainties.

An initial uncertainty is whether Cohen attempts to self-induce a mystical experience in the act of literary creation, or to recreate in words a prior moment of mystical vision. While the latter possibility might seem the most likely path, and the one followed by other mystically inclined writers from William Blake to Christina Rossetti, Cohen's own comments about the novel suggest otherwise. In an interview with Michael Harris, he indicates that *Beautiful Losers* was 'a life and death effort' to get himself out of the hole of depression:

I felt it was the end. But it was the only thing I could do. There was nothing I could do. I said to myself if I can't blacken these pages, then I really can't do anything.[3]

Cohen further relates that, even though 'when I wrote *Beautiful Losers* I thought

I was completely broken and on the edge of redemption,'[4] the state of mind expressed in the book was prophetic of his own worsening state a year or two later.

Thus it would appear that *Beautiful Losers* is an attempt to work his way through despair toward a transcendent experience of life. Like so many mystics before him, Cohen pushes to the extreme edge in his dark night of the soul, seemingly attempting to follow the familiar pathway down towards a way up. In *Beautiful Losers* Cohen suggests that such extremes are prerequisites of ultimate beatitude. 'F' proclaims that

A saint is someone who has achieved a remote human possibility. It is impossible to say what that possibility is. I think it has something to do with the energy of love. Contact with this energy results in the exercise of a kind of balance in the chaos of existence. A saint does not dissolve the chaos; if he did the world would have changed long ago. I do not think that a saint dissolves the chaos even for himself, for there is something arrogant and warlike in the notion of a man setting the universe in order. It is a kind of balance that is his glory. He drives the drifts like an escaped ski. His course is the caress of a hill. (p 121)

In *Beautiful Losers* we see many of the characters riding the drifts to the extreme edge, which Cohen, like Robert Browning, suggests to be the way of vision. None of them is a 'normal' or average person. 'I' is a frustrated historian, as constipated in his writing as in his body. He is the husband of Edith, a pock-marked member of the 'A' tribe of Indians, whose body becomes an instrument for sexual extremes and who commits suicide by sitting under an elevator. 'F' is a French-Canadian, Jewish, member of parliament, and violent revolutionary, as well as the provider of sexual thrills for 'I,' Edith, and the nurse who tends him on his syphilitic deathbed. Catherine Tekakwitha, the subject of 'I' 's research, is a seventeenth-century Indian girl who suffers extreme agonies of self-deprivation and torture as an early Canadian, Christian martyr. Perhaps the most unusual or extreme figure of all is the unnamed hero in the final section of the book. He is a hermit, reported for molesting small boys, who in the end returns to the city and turns into a Ray Charles movie.

It is possible to see this final 'saintly' figure as the embodiment of new possibility, the 'if' of an integrated personality resulting from unification of 'I' and 'F.' Accordingly, 'I' is not really a character, but symbolic of the ego or rational side of the psyche, and 'F' represents the world of the id. Indeed all the characters may be seen as fantasy figures, rather than actual human beings. Such an interpretation would happily fit with Cohen's comments about the book as a working out of his inner torments.

Whether or not one accepts Cohen's preoccupation with 'saintly' extremists as part of a broadly religious approach to existence, the attitudes expressed in *Beautiful Losers* seemingly have much in common with those of mystics through the ages. Although some evidence for this seemingly mystical approach is gleaned from 'I' 's reaction to 'F' and from the behaviour of the hero of the final section, most of it is supplied by 'F.' His lessons to 'I' form the core of the philosophic or didactic thought in the novel.

The first conventional mystical attitude has to do with a sense of the unity of being, and an acceptance of everything as part of an overall harmony. 'F' maintains that all matter is holy, an understanding which belongs to the North American Indian and which partly explains the central place of the Indian in the story. 'F' 's advice to 'fuck a saint' is a plea to reunite the estranged partnership of body and soul, and his continued emphasis on sexual delights is an attempt to counteract the Calvinist-Jansenist repression of the same. He reacts against the prevalent practical if not theoretical dualism which has led the North American white man in particular to regard his body with embarrassment or guilt. In a broader sense, he may be reacting, like Norman O. Brown, against the whole Christian concept of the fall, in which man clothed his body with shame after expulsion from the garden.[5] He may be seeking a return to paradisal innocence. In any case, 'F' 's acceptance of all existence leads him to maintain there are never any dirty objects nor dirty words. To 'I' 's query, 'Do you think I can learn to perceive the diamond of good amongst all the shit,' 'F' replies, 'It is all diamond.'

Acceptance of all the universe as a unity also means acceptance of all that has passed. This involves rejecting the historian's fragmentation of history into neat numerical periods. 'F,' like the Indian, sees all time contained in the present and bemoans to 'I,' 'What a hunchback History and the Past have made of your body.' The extreme of such acceptance involves the genocide of the Second World War, and 'F' makes this symbolic gesture of acceptance in the joyful bath he has with Edith. Lathering themselves with a bar of soap made from human corpses symbolically implies gathering into themselves past deeds as part of the unity of being. 'F' sees the immersion as a baptism into a new innocence.

Such a mystical sense of unity is gained through a reliance on emotional and intuitive perception rather than rationality. Clearly man's emphasis on rational sequence or logic is under attack by 'F,' who shouts to 'I,' 'Connect nothing. Place things side by side on your arborite table, if you must, but connect nothing.' 'I,' the rational thinker who is logically trying to piece together the facts of history, comes to realize that

I want to be consumed by unreason. I want to be swept along ... I want 'F' 's experiences, his emotional extravagance. (p 58)

'F' 's reaction against rational thought and abstract classification is apparent in his suspicion of naming:

Science begins in coarse naming, a willingness to disregard the particular shape and the destiny of each red life and call them all Rose. To a more brutal, more active 'I,' all flowers look alike, like Negroes and Chinamen. (p 51)

The trick is to name without naming; that is, to name with the emotions rather than the mind, which 'F' attempts with his mystical chants in which objects and names are used as a kind of invocation or a prayer of being. Names become magic rather than labels. 'F' wants himself to be a new kind of Jew, a Moses-magician, leading his people away from the old concept of law and towards a new land of magic – in which religious experience, sex, and art are all equal elements.

Another aspect of the mystical concept of unity of being is the desire to lose the self in that unity, that is, to discard the ego as the source of separation between self and others. For 'F,' both Catherine and Edith are examples of this loss of self, the first through the ecstasy of her religious life, the second through the sexual ecstasy attained in the Danish vibrator scene. Similarly, the hero of the final section achieves 'F' 's goal to 'be magic' rather than a magician by dissolving into the movie screen and becoming a reflective surface for the energy of the world. The story finishes with the audience realizing he is 'making it' as the founder of magic Canada and the new Jew:

At that point where he is most absent, that's when the gasps started, because the future screams through that point, going both ways. (p 305)

Nevertheless, despite the message of success at the end of *Beautiful Losers*, and despite the similarity between 'F' 's views and those espoused by many mystics, the final impression is not one of mystical experience fully realized, but only preached. Like 'F,' Cohen attempts to be a Moses leading us out of the bondage of our dualistic, rationalistic attitudes, but he never reaches the promised mystic land. Rather, his efforts at mystical magic increasingly seem grotesque illusions.

There are several reasons why Cohen's mystical pretensions appear unrealized. The first has to do with his treatment of evil. The true mystic in the Judao-Christian tradition does not disregard evil, but works through it. Cohen, on the other hand, seems unwilling to grapple fully with the problem of evil, a problem that cannot be whisked away by nice thoughts. Merely saying that a saint is someone who 'so loves the world that he gives himself to the laws of gravity and chance,' and who 'can love the shapes of human beings, the fine and twisted shapes of the heart,' glosses over the hard facts. Unlike some of his earlier poems which grapple with the problem of historical evils, Cohen seems too ready to accept the past as part of the unity of being. The scene with the human soap is a case in point. Hitler's practice of genocide is obviously a horrifying fact of history. When the issue is placed in the comic context of the waiter and the bar of soap, the result is grotesque black humour.

Sandra Djwa is critical of such horror presented as an absurdity, which she sees as an 'attempt to exorcise evil by filtering it through the comic mode.'[6] Yet if Cohen were attempting to suggest a condition of human meaninglessness and estrangement from value, or simply presenting an apocalyptic vision, such an alliance of humour and horror would be extremely effective, and in the same descriptive-grotesque pattern as Joseph Heller's *Catch 22* or the movie MASH.

Cohen's purpose is apparently quite different. He seems to be saying that this grotesque combination of humour and horror is indeed holy. The grotesque does not indirectly point to the sublime, as William Van O'Connor and others maintain, but indeed it *is* the sublime.

Such an equation seems in itself inadvertently grotesque, and Cohen's effort to make his point in an artistically interesting way increases the grotesqueness. Cohen wants us to see that everything in life is 'kosher.' Yet he is well aware that the glorious message that life is beautiful can make boring or trite literature. In order to push beyond the platitude, Cohen must show that those things which usually we do not regard as beautiful and good are indeed so. He must seek out, dramatize, and exaggerate conventional vices or taboos, while shouting a resounding 'yes.' At times the bond between the moral and the exemplum becomes so distanced that one or another is stretched to distortion.

Another reason for suggesting that *Beautiful Losers* falls short of the truly mystical grotesque has to do with the mystical notion of impersonality. Cohen suggests that Edith's loss of self in her sexual ecstasy is a kind of saintliness, and that 'F' has made her beautiful in leading her to these heights. There remains, however, an inescapable element of sadism in the liaison, of cruel sexual exploitation of the woman which no amount of poetic praise of 'the energy of love' or mystical statement of loss equalling gain can transform. Is Edith's self-loss really her gain, or is it merely 'F' 's? To suggest that Edith's suicide by squashing herself under the elevator is the ultimate sacrifice seems a distortion of mystical insight. The same can be said for the masochism evident in Cohen's reconstruction of the Catherine Tekakwitha story.

It may be argued that this kind of logic can be applied only to realistic characters and not to figures in a fantasy. Yet however 'unreal' they may be, or however much they are fantastic projections of the unconscious, their actions are connected to human experience and to Cohen's vision of human life. As such they lend themselves to analysis and interpretation. In certain instances the critic's relation to grotesque fantasy may be that of a psychoanalyst to a dream. In the case of *Beautiful Losers*, whether these fantastic experiences are viewed literally or symbolically, they seem more sado-masochistic than mystic.

Thus one comes to the question of whether Cohen's mystical inclination is at bottom really a spiritual interest. Cohen himself has admitted that his attraction to the saintly life as he sees it is 'not because [it's] ascetic, but because it's aesthetic.'[7] At the same time, he mentions his interest in the misfits and 'oddities' of society:

I always loved the people the world used to call mad. I always loved people who were somehow aberrated, who seemed to be aberrated from the alleged normal. I used to hang out in Phillips Square and talk to those old men and I used to hang out at Northeastern Lunch that was down on Clark Street, or with junkies.[8]

Such comments suggest that Cohen's loving embrace of aberrations and extremists as spiritual models – the masochist as martyr, the 'pervert' as prophet, the suicide as saint – is simply an artist's fascination with ugliness as rare beauty.

Sandra Djwa puts Cohen in the *fin de siècle* tradition of decadent romanticism. She suggests that his immersion in destruction is partially 'savoured'; that his decent into darkness and evil is a source of pleasure as well as pain. Cohen's second novel may well follow Oscar Wilde, who valued the disintegrative process as a form of art. The grotesque for Cohen may simply send out aesthetic rather than spiritual vibrations, as the title 'Beautiful Losers' suggests.

Of course these two concerns, the spiritual and the aesthetic, are not mutually exclusive, and the obvious way out of such an either-or proposition is the romantic notion that the true artist, by his attempt to find new revelations beneath the dull surface of normal appearances, is a kind of religious visionary or mystic. The temptation is to 'mistake catalogued sensation for new revelation.'[9] *Beautiful Losers* at times seems to have fallen heir to the indulgence and sensationalism of Swinburne's *Lesbia Brandon*, with which it has many similarities.

Northrop Frye comments on the modern 'cult of the holy sinner' in literature, a cult which focuses on

The person who achieves an exceptional awareness, whether religious or ascetic in character, from acts of cruelty, or, at least, bring about such an awareness in us.[10]

Cohen's beautiful losers, especially 'F,' would seem to fit into this category of holy sinner or grotesque saint. Yet Frye connects this cult with a sadist vision of nature:

According to this, nature teaches us that pleasure is the highest good in life, and the keenest form of pleasure consists in inflicting or suffering pain. Hence the real natural society would not be the reign of equality and reason prophesied by Rousseau; it would be a society in which those who liked tormenting others were set free to do so. [11]

Cohen's figures may talk and act like Frye's holy sinners, but Cohen seemingly would set himself on the side of Rousseau rather than de Sade. The beautiful loser, he suggests, is a messiah of mystic bliss.

Yet ultimately Cohen fails to convince, and this failure suggests that *Beautiful Losers* moves toward the mystical grotesque without achieving it. The artist-magician does not fully succeed with his magic. Instead of the way up, Cohen leaves us with the way down towards sado-masochistic extremism. Despite the mystic message, the horrible-humorous mix is not transformed into holiness. The grotesque alone remains in the eyes of the beholder.

Conclusion

Clearly the Canadian writers who have chosen gothic modes are not isolated or idiosyncratic. The gothic tradition, adopted and adapted in this country in the nineteenth century, has continued strong in the twentieth, and among both English and French Canadians it shows no sign of waning. Moreover, its persistence is matched by its diversity. The varieties of gothic and grotesque fiction we have examined indicate that the gothic route is not a rut, and that most often convention consorts with individuality. Nevertheless there are common features, and some of these illustrate Canadian gothicism as a whole. When the particular works are viewed as a group, a pattern emerges which, while not necessarily unique to Canadian fiction, appears to have some distinctive aspects or emphases.

The most basic of all gothic motifs – the awareness of death – is obviously central to the books in this study. In the nineteenth-century romances particularly, there is often the menace of violent, physical death. This motif is also present to a lesser extent in *La Guerre, Yes Sir!* and *Cocksure*, but twentieth-century works are apt to emphasize psychological or spiritual rather than corporal death. *Kamouraska* and *Surfacing* suggest a kind of psychological disintegration or paralysis leading to a death-in-life existence. In *Beautiful Losers*, psychological death is connected to spiritual death, whereas in *The Double Hook* and *Mad Shadows* the spiritual emphasis exists by itself.

A second basic motif of gothicism is the preoccupation with evil. A particularly interesting feature of much of the fiction in this study is the insistence upon evil despite an abandonment of any explicit religious dimension, and occasionally despite the presence of anti-religious sentiment. It seems that for a number of modern Canadian writers, God may be dead but the devil lives on. Characters in both French and English works are forever confronting manifestations of a primal evil which goes beyond behaviourist or sociological explanations. The depictions of the Starmaker in *Cocksure*, Caleb Gare in *Wild Geese*, and Elisabeth Rolland in *Kamouraska* all point to a mysterious darkness or evil at the very roots of the human condition. Even Margaret Atwood, who comes closest of all the writers discussed to providing a sociological (and partially psychological) rationale for human wrongs, still recognizes an innate power of cruelty and evil. It is perhaps indicative of Canadian character that in *Beautiful Losers* Leonard Cohen's attempt at a kind of mystical transformation of evil fails.

Another important aspect of evil in the fiction analyzed is the overpowering force of human will. In both the nineteenth- and the twentieth century works, we find that the dominance of one human over another is a prime contribution to the final doom or destructive action of the story. Leslie Fiedler has suggested that the pattern of relationships in all gothic tales can largely be explained in Freudian terms as having sexual origins. Yet it is evident in Canadian gothic fiction at least that the sexual encounters or conflicts are more often the result than the cause of the wilful desire for domination. Whether one considers the obsessive attitudes of Wacousta and Colonel de Haldimar, or the destructiveness of Caleb Gare and the Starmaker, or the subtler forms of domination exhibited by Elisabeth Rolland both as a young and an older woman, it is apparent that sexual power is only one element in the gothic protagonist's urge to control or manipulate other people.

The menace of death and evil are major constituents in the pervasive atmosphere of fear or horror present in all the works in this study. Such an atmosphere is, of course, the *sine qua non* of gothic fiction, whether in the old 'tale-of-terror' tradition or in the half-humorous, grotesque mode of much modern literature. However, a persistent feature of the fear or horror in many Canadian gothic works is the sense of threat to or collapse of an entire culture. *For My Country* and *La Guerre, Yes Sir!* are but two examples of a repeated pattern in nineteenth- and twentieth-century Canadian fiction. Margaret Atwood's comment about our heroes – that 'the pull of the native tradition is not in the direction of individual heroes at all, but rather in the direction of collective heroes'[1] – may be applied to our failures or misfortunes as well. In Canadian gothic fiction, although a sense of menace is sometimes focused in an individual's fear, it very often has a collective reference.

Moreover a pattern of *double* menace continues through much of the fiction. The dual dangers of both natural and civilized life are sometimes expressed in the nineteenth-century fiction as a contrast between different types of people. Thus in Richardson's romance there is a contrast and conflict between the 'civilized' Colonel de Haldimar and the 'natural' Wacousta, just as in *Le Chercheur de trésors* there is a contrast between the scientific ways of the students and the primitive attitude of Amand. By comparison in the twentieth-century works, the dichotomy between nature and civilization is usually presented as a conflict internalized in one character; for example, there is the double interior life of Madame Rolland in *Kamouraska* and the disturbing alternatives pressing upon the narrator in *Surfacing*.

Whatever the reasons for and implications of gothic and grotesque literature – and many have been suggested in this study – the vision it presents is of a world beyond material surfaces. By taking us into mysterious spiritual and psychological realms, gothic writers have provided an alternative to the more familiar paths of realistic writers; at the very least they have helped prevent Canadian fiction from becoming homogeneously 'cramped by rationalism and bleached by exposure to unvarying daylight.'[2]

Although gothic fiction moves away from realistic social analysis by its imaginative exploration of the numinous and the depths of primitive emotion, there still appears to be some connection between gothicism and the culture from which it springs. Despite the problems involved in relating literary genres or modes to history, many critics, as discussed earlier, nonetheless maintain that gothic and grotesque varieties of expression are turned to in periods of cultural decay or disorder. Where Varma sees all gothicism as a 'response to the political and religious insecurity of disturbed times,'[3] other critics, such as Kayser and Lawson, find the grotesque mode in particular related to cultural death and disintegration. Certainly the widespread sense of cultural disorder felt in the twentieth century, and the resurgence of gothic fiction of the grotesque variety especially, seem more than coincidental phenomena.

One wonders, therefore, whether a return to cultural stability would cause gothic and grotesque literature to fade from the scene. It has been suggested that 'should men once again generally agree upon what reality is, the grotesque mode should theoretically once again lapse into disuse.'[4] However, in the absence of a cultural frame of reality or stability of meaning, we can only speculate upon the likelihood.

There is another possibility. Perhaps by probing beneath the surface of life, gothic and grotesque literature helps engender a fresh frame of meaning. Perhaps its strange and disturbing configurations of experience contribute to the reordering of our perceptions which, many would argue, is at the base of cultural revitalization. The very energy of much gothic and grotesque fiction supports a connection with cultural vitality as much as with cultural mortality. This being the case, those works studied which appear so death-ridden and frequently disintegrative may indeed be considered catalysts of regeneration. With good reason we may suppose that in culture, as in the natural world, death and decay are compost for new growth.

Notes

INTRODUCTION

1 A good example of this approach is Ronald Sutherland's *Second Image: Comparative Studies in Quebec/Canadian Literature* (Toronto 1971).

2 Margaret Atwood, *Survival: A Thematic Guide to Canadian Literature* (Toronto 1972); D.G. Jones, *Butterfly on Rock: A Study of Themes and Images in Canadian Literature* (Toronto 1970)

3 Devendra P. Varma's *The Gothic Flame: A History of the Gothic Novel in England* (London 1957) is the most useful study of the gothic and my discussion of the term owes much to his research.

4 *Ibid.* 129

5 John Ruskin, *The Stones of Venice* II, ch. 6 (London 1906)

6 Leslie A. Fiedler, *Love and Death in the American Novel*, rev. ed. (New York 1969) 118

7 Varma, *The Gothic Flame* 224 Mario Praz's view in *The Romantic Agony* (New York 1933) that the romantic period was characterized by algolagnia, that is, by sexual pleasure obtained through pain, prompts Montague Summers's comment, quoted by Varma: 'it is probable that something of this masochistic feeling lies (perhaps quite unconsciously) at the root of the fascination so universally exercised by uncanny tales of ghosts and spectres, which send hearers to bed shuddering and glancing over their shoulders with delicious apprehension of supernatural visitants.'

8 In his critical essay, 'The Northanger Novels,' Michael Sadlier states that the gothic romance was 'as much an expression of a deep subversive impulse as [was] the French Revolution' (quoted in Varma 398). Fiedler maintains that 'the guilt which underlies the gothic and motivates its thought is the guilt of the revolutionary haunted by the [paternal] past which he has been striving to destroy (Fiedler 115).

9 Frances K. Barasch has traced the history in *The Grotesque: A Study in Meanings* (The Hague 1971), and this synopsis is especially indebted to her research. Wolfgang Kayser's *The Grotesque in Art and Literature*, translated from the German by Ulrich Weisstein (New York 1966), also provides a history of the term and an intensive and useful study of European grotesque art and literature, but it has comparatively little to say about English and American art and literature. As well, see Arthur Clayborough, *The Grotesque in English Literature* (Oxford 1965) 11.

10 For example, in 1686 Sir Thomas Browne maintained that 'there are no grotesques in nature.' *Works* (quoted in Clayborough 3)

11 In 1718 Charles Gilden condemned the fact that 'in all the fine Arts indeed there has a *grotesque* and *gothique* taste prevailed, which relishes everything that is not natural' (quoted in Barasch 97). Of special interest is the early association of the grotesque with the gothic. Addison spoke of a taste for the grotesque as 'a gothic manner in writing.' *The Spectator* (quoted in Clayborough 11) Often both terms were ascribed by critics to the tragicomic 'irregularities' of Renaissance writers.

12 Samuel Taylor Coleridge, *Lectures and Notes on Shakespeare and Other English Poets* (London 1821; collected and edited by T. Ashe, London 1900). Coleridge saw the grotesque as an uncommon juxtaposition or oddity for its own sake, and since it lacked a moral or transcendental quality, he considered it a form of false humour. Coleridge continued the earlier association of the grotesque with comic indecorum and vulgarity, while avoiding any condemnation. Although Coleridge denied the term grotesque to the sublime and moral humour of fantastic allegory, by his perception of the transcendental quality in true humour he encouraged later writers to 'see the potential sublimity of the grotesque, to perceive within fantastic comedy the idea of the soul, and to understand the satirical grotesque as a "protective device" shielding human terror and high moral indignation.' Thus a modern critic such as Erich Auerbach refers to fantastic allegory as grotesque satire.

13 Ruskin, *The Stones of Venice*, III, ch. 3

14 Kayser, see especially pp 179-89.

15 Flannery O'Connor, *Mystery and Manners*, ed. Sally and Robert Fitzgerald (New York 1969) 33-4

16 The German critic and writer, Thomas Mann, associates the grotesque with tragicomedy when he says, 'for I feel that, bodily and essentially, the striking feature of modern art is that it has ceased to recognize the categories of tragic and comic, or the dramatic classifications, tragedy and comedy. It sees life as tragicomedy, with the result that the grotesque is its most genuine style – to the extent, indeed, that today that is the only guise in which the

sublime may appear' (quoted in William Van O'Connor, *The Grotesque: An American Genre and Other Essays* (Carbondale; Ill. 1962) 3. Still another critic Karl Guthke, makes a distinction between the tragicomic and the grotesque absurd (*Modern Tragicomedy* [New York 1966] 73-4).

17 Originally connected in eighteenth-century criticism, both continued to be connected or given similar characteristics by modern critics. Thus Ihad Hassan defines the gothicism of Carson McCullers as an 'interest in the grotesque, the freakish and the incongruous.' *Radical Innocence: The Contemporary American Novel* (Princeton 1961) 202. The pattern of fiction from the American South, described as grotesque by William Van O'Connor, is referred to as 'New American Gothic' by Irving Malin in *New American Gothic* (Carbondale 1962).

CHAPTER 1 Early Gothic

1 René Wellek and Austin Warren, *Theory of Literature*, 3rd ed. (New York 1962) 216
2 In *Love and Death in the American Novel* Fiedler provides a discussion of gothic and sentimental romances, to which this analysis is much indebted.
3 Quoted in Wellek and Warren, *Theory of Literature* 8
4 Ramsay Cook, *The Maple Leaf Forever: Essays on Nationalism and Politics in Canada* (Toronto 1971) 113
5 François-Xavier Garneau, *Histoire du Canada*, 5th ed. (Paris 1920)
6 Cook, *The Maple Leaf Forever* 113
7 Kenneth N. Windsor, 'Historical Writing in Canada to 1920,' *Literary History of Canada: Canadian Literature in English*, revised edition, I, 222-64
8 Frances Parkman, *France and England in North America*, 7 vols, 1865-92, quoted in 'Historical Writings in Canada,' *Literary History of Canada*, I, 247
9 Jean Rigeault, 'Le Conte au Québec,' *Canadian Literature* 53 (Summer 1972) 60-80. The tale of 'La Jongleuse,' for instance, is an example of a deliberate attempt at final reassurance, following a story of unsurpassed horror in which the Indian is the devil incarnate. After describing 'un de ces actes d'atrocité incroyables que les sauvages d'Amérique commirant si souvent contre les Pionniers de la Foi et de la Civilisation' (p 205), the narrator concludes by advising his listeners to respond to the plaints of the doomed La Jongleuse with prayers: 'disons-lui un ave maria' (p 289), and then, he implies, all will be well.
10 H.-R. Casgrain, 'La Jongleuse,' *Soirées canadiennes: Recueil de littérature nationale* (Quebec 1861) 205-89

11 J.-C. Taché, *Forestiers et voyageurs: Moeurs et légendes canadiennes* (Montreal 1884)
12 Jack Warwick, *The Long Journey: Literary Themes of French Canada* (Toronto 1968)
13 Philippe-Joseph Aubert de Gaspé, *The Canadians of Old*, trans. Charles G. D. Roberts (New York 1890). First published as *Les Anciens Canadiens* (Quebec 1863)
14 Joseph-Etienne-Eugène Marmette, *François de Bienville*, 4th ed. (Montreal 1924)
15 Joseph Doutre, *Les Fiancés de 1812* (Montreal 1969)
16 Pamphile Lemay, *Les Vengeances*, 3rd ed. (Montreal 1930)
17 Gilbert Parker, *The Seats of the Mighty* (London 1896)
18 Gilbert Parker, *When Valmond Came to Pontiac* (Chicago 1895)

CHAPTER 2 Canadian Prototype: *Wacousta*

1 Published in book form in 1832 (Brockville) after an initial appearance as a serial in 1826 and 1827
2 For the reason given in the introduction, this study will use only readily available editions for its analyses. In the case of *Wacousta*, this means that all quotations refer to *Wacousta; or, The Prophecy* with an introduction by Carl F. Klinck (Toronto 1967).

The first edition was published anonymously in three volumes as *Wacousta; A Tale of the Canadas* (London 1833). Of interest also when it may be obtained is an early twentieth-century edition with illustrations by Charles W. Jeffreys: *Wacousta; A Tale of the Pontiac Conspiracy* (Toronto 1902).

The recent edition is abridged to three-quarters the original size. The main omissions, as discussed by Carl Klinck in his introduction, involve some prolonged sentimental scenes with Charles de Haldimar and the various heroines, and reminiscences by various other characters, particularly the officers, of past activities. The reminiscences apparently are designed to provide a different perspective upon events, but seem to the modern reader to slow the pace unnecessarily.

Worth mentioning also, since they relate to this analysis, are the omissions of some descriptions of sexual excitement, as, for example, in the soldiers' reaction (in chapter 7 of the original edition) to the exposure of Ellen Holloway's 'white and polished bosom.' The recounting of de Haldimar's chaste embrace with the passionate Oucanasta (in chapter 18 of the original edition), provides further evidence of Richardson's quick check upon a mounting atmosphere of sexuality. Although Oucanasta's sexual interest in the white man is touched upon only briefly in the original edition, it is completely omitted from the recent edition.

3 *Wacousta* xvii-xviii
4 Carl F. Klinck, 'The Canadas 1812-1841,' *Literary History of Canada*, I, 151
5 *Ibid.* 152
6 Richardson fought as a young volunteer in the British army in the War of 1812, and was held prisoner after the capture of Moraviantown by the Americans in 1813, when the renowned Indian leader Tecumseh was killed.
7 Leslie A. Fiedler, *Love and Death in the American Novel* 97
8 John Moss discusses the sexual patterns of *Wacousta* in *Patterns of Isolation in English-Canadian Fiction* (Toronto 1974) 46-9.
9 Of course the villains of many non-gothic works – such as Don Juan or Richardson's Lovelace – are permitted a developed sexuality also.
10 Carl F. Klinck, introduction to *Wacousta* xii
11 Northrop Frye, 'Conclusion,' *Literary History of Canada*, II, 342
12 Nietzsche and Freud might have argued that this exorcism is what *all* literature attempts. Nonetheless, the degree of demonic or unconscious darkness revealed in gothic literature surely is greater than many other kinds of fiction.

CHAPTER 3 Decorative Gothic: *The Golden Dog*

1 In this discussion the text used will be William Kirby, FRSC, *The Golden Dog (Le Chien d'or): A Romance of Old Quebec* (Toronto 1969). This recent edition, abridged from the original 1877 edition of 678 pages, omits chapters which hinder the flow of the narrative, or serve only to add more details of local life. Derek Crawley discusses the 'minimum loss of the artistry, atmosphere and narrative' resulting from this abridgement in his introduction to the NCL edition.
2 Desmond Pacey, *Creative Writing in Canada*, rev. ed. (Toronto 1961) 75
3 Frye, 'Conclusion,' *Literary History of Canada*, II, 353
4 James MacPherson Le Moine, *Maple Leaves: Canadian History, Literature* (Quebec 1863-94)
5 W. Kirby, FRSC, 'A Biographical Sketch of the Author of *Maple Leaves*,' in James Le Moine, *Maple Leaves*, 6th Series (1863)
6 Fiedler, *Love and Death in the American Novel* 149
7 *Ibid.* 115
8 *Ibid.* 118
9 Varma, *The Gothic Flame* 218
10 Philippe-Joseph Aubert de Gaspé, *Les Anciens Canadiens* (Quebec 1863)

CHAPTER 4 Towards the Grotesque: *Le Chercheur de trésors*

1 Philippe-Ignace-François Aubert de Gaspé, *Le Chercheur de trésors* ou *L'Influence d'un livre* (Montreal 1968). First published in 1837
2 See, for example, 'François Marois alias Malouin alias Lepage,' *Le Bulletin des recherches historiques* XLIX (1943) 79-102, which gives the origin of the murderer Mareuil; and Joseph-Edmond Roy, *Histoire de la seigneurie de Larison* (Lévis 1897-1904) IV, 205-6, on la mère Nollette of Beaumont. In a biographical sketch of the senior Aubert de Gaspé, Luc Lacourcière observes that the son's knowledge of the customs and anecdotes of the times could only have been learned from his father. *Dictionary of Canadian Biography*, ed. Marc La Terreur (Toronto 1972) X, 18-22
3 Léopold Leblanc, preface to *Le Chercheur de trésors* i-vii
4 Quoted in William Van O'Connor, *The Grotesque* 5

CHAPTER 5 Gothic Propaganda: *For My Country: Pour la patrie*

1 Speaking of Garneau's *Histoire*, Ramsay Cook remarks that it was in this source with its story of a glorious past 'that French Canada's first literary flowering took root.' *The Maple Leaf Forever* 119. See also Gérard Tougas, *History of French Canadian Literature*, 2nd ed., trans. Alta Lind Cook (Toronto 1966).
2 J.P. Tardivel, *For My Country: Pour la patrie*, trans. by Sheila Fischman, with an introduction by A. I. Silver (Toronto 1975). First published in *La Vérité* XV 2 (August 1895)
3 Tougas, *History of French-Canadian Literature* 54

CHAPTER 6 Modern Gothic

1 Kayser, *The Grotesque in Art and Literature* 188
2 Kenneth Burke, *Attitudes towards History*, quoted in Lawson, 'The Grotesque in Recent Southern Fiction' 171
3 *Ibid.* 176
4 Margaret Atwood contends in *Survival* that Canadian writing generally is pre-occupied with victims, but I think this is less the case in English Canada than in French Canada.
5 See Ronald Sutherland, 'The Calvinist-Jansenist Pantomime,' *Second Image* (Toronto 1971) 60-87.
6 Lawson 'The Grotesque in Recent Southern Fiction' 175
7 *Ibid.* 176

8 This distinction has some resemblance to Clayborough's system of classification, which in turn is based on Jung's distinction between the mind's background or regressive movement, which satisfies the demands of the unconscious, and its forward movement or profession, which satisfies the conscious. Clayborough links this polarization to a distinction between dream or fantasy thinking and direct thinking, and suggests that intentionally grotesque art may take either of these directions.

CHAPTER 7 Psychological Gothic: *Kamouraska*

1 Anne Hébert, *Kamouraska*, translation by Norman Shapiro (Toronto 1973)
2 William Van O'Connor, *The Grotesque* 18
3 *Ibid.* 17
4 Margaret Atwood, Afterword to *The Journals of Susanna Moodie* (Toronto 1970) 62
5 O'Connor, *The Grotesque* 18

CHAPTER 8 Sociological Gothic: *Wild Geese* and *Surfacing*

1 Martha Ostenso, *Wild Geese*, with introduction by Carlyle King (Toronto 1961)
2 Margaret Atwood, *Surfacing* (Toronto 1972)
3 Carlyle King, introduction to *Wild Geese* ix
4 Margaret Atwood in *Survival* discusses the recurring motif of the family as prison in Canadian literature. Though family life at the Gares does repress all spontaneity and joy in the children, it is evident that farm work and the father's wilful attempt to keep her at it are a contributing source of Judith's anger. When Lind offers Judith the admired amber beads, the latter rejects them since 'Wouldn't I look funny with them on! Specially, cleaning the stables' (p 18). Perhaps her dislike of farming has something to do with the beauty it seems to deny.
5 George Grant, *Technology and Empire: Perspectives on North America* (Toronto 1969)

CHAPTER 9 Terrible Grotesque: *Mad Shadows*

1 Marie-Claire Blais, *Mad Shadows*, translation by Merloyd Lawrence, with introduction by Naïm Kattan (Toronto 1971). Originally published as *La Belle Bête* (Paris 1959)
2 Cf. *Le Chercheur de trésors.*

3 See introduction to this book.

4 Kayser, *The Grotesque in Art and Literature* 57

5 Lawson, 'The Grotesque in Recent Southern Fiction' 172

6 See Kayser, *The Grotesque in Art and Literature* 21-2.

7 D.W. Robertson, Jr has demonstrated that in Chaucer and much of medieval literature physical description is essentially symbolic, and each physical attribute helps to place a character somewhere on a scale of which the two poles are *caritas* and *cupiditas*. *A Preface to Chaucer: Studies in Medieval Perspectives* (Princeton 1969)

8 Kayser states that this sense of an abyss is characteristic of the grotesque, and thus he contrasts it to the gothic mode where 'the abysmal forces are integrated with an order that is all the stronger for being able to contain such ominous elements' (p 141). However, the abyss, both actual and symbolic, which exists in such gothic works as *Wacousta* is evidence that such a distinction is not always viable.

9 Sherwood Anderson, *Winesburg, Ohio* (New York 1958) 25

10 Malin, *New American Gothic* 14-49

11 William Van O'Connor, *The Grotesque* 18

12 Translated by Joyce Marshall in the English edition

13 Quoted in Lawson, 'The Grotesque in Recent Southern Fiction' 173

14 Flannery O'Connor *Mystery and Manners* 34

15 Ruskin, *The Stones of Venice* III, 129

16 *Ibid.* 131

17 Hassan, as well as Ruskin, subscribes to this view.

CHAPTER 10 Sportive Grotesque: *La Guerre, Yes Sir!*

1 Roch Carrier, *La Guerre, Yes Sir!*, translation by Sheila Fischman (Toronto 1970). First published by Éditions du Jour (Montreal 1968)

2 Writing about *La Guerre, Yes Sir!*, René Dionne states that the humour largely lies in the disproportion between the characters' psychological or social stature and their actual situation. 'La Guerre, Yes Sir,' *Relations* 331 (1968) 279-81

3 When discussing the base or false grotesque in which 'grossness, of one kind or another, is, indeed, an unfailing characteristic of the style' (III, 137), Ruskin mentions, as an example of abominable detail, a carving at Santa Maria Formosa in which 'the *teeth* are represented as *decayed*.' However, the decayed teeth of Carrier's 'saintly' nun do not indicate the diminutive power of the author's mind, as Ruskin would have it, but rather indicate the unhealthy attitudes of the purveyors of religion, while possibly satirizing the

vacuous pink and white statuettes ensconsed in households and in whose image the villagers attempt to place Esmalda.

4 Atwood *Survival* 220
5 Nancy Bailey, 'The Corriveau Wake: Carrier's Celebration of Life,' *Journal of Canadian Fiction* III (Summer 1972) 43-7
6 Carrier used this phrase in a seminar at York University.
7 Anderson, *Winesburg, Ohio* 25
8 Ronald Sutherland, 'La Guerre, Yes Sir!,' *Canadian Literature* 40 (1969) 85-6
9 Robertson, *A Preface to Chaucer* 252
10 *Ibid.* 253
11 Charles Muscatine, *Chaucer and the French Tradition* (Berkeley 1969) 246
12 Ronald Sutherland, 'Faulknerian Quebec,' *Canadian Literature* 40 (1969) 85-6
13 Malcolm Cowley, introduction to William Faulkner, *The Portable Faulkner* (New York 1967) xxi
14 William Faulkner, 'Nobel Prize Address,' *The Portable Faulkner* 724
15 Ruskin, *The Stones of Venice* III, 141

CHAPTER 11 Symbolic Grotesque: *The Double Hook*

1 Sheila Watson, *The Double Hook*, with introduction by John Grube (Toronto 1969), New Canadian Library, No. 54. First published in 1959
2 Quoted in Malin, *New American Gothic* 8
3 Flannery O'Connor, *Mystery and Manners* 33-4
4 Anderson, *Winesburg, Ohio* 25
5 Leslie Monkman, 'Coyote as Trickster in *The Double Hook,' Canadian Literature* 52 (Spring 1972) 70-5
6 It also appears to be strongly influenced by T.S. Eliot.

CHAPTER 12 Satiric Grotesque: *Cocksure*

1 Kayser, *The Grotesque in Art and Literature* 37
2 *Ibid.* 174
3 *Ibid.* 186
4 *Ibid.* 173
5 Northrop Frye, *Anatomy of Criticism: Four Essays* (New York 1969) 225
6 *Ibid.* 224
7 Mordecai Richler, *Cocksure* (Toronto 1968)
8 In his discussion of *Cocksure*, George Woodcock distinguishes between these two levels of satire, a distinction which is worth developing in this analysis of the grotesque. *Mordecai Richler* (Toronto 1970) 52

9 David Worcester, *The Art of Satire* (New York 1960) 106
10 Wolfgang Kayser gives this recounting of Weiland's classification in *The Grotesque in Art and Literature* 30.
11 Woodcock 52
12 Warren Tallman, 'Wolf In the Snow,' in *A Choice of Critics*, edited by George Woodcock (Oxford University Press 1966)
13 Worcester, 107
14 *Ibid*. 108
15 Nathan Cohen, 'A Conversation with Mordecai Richler,' *Tamarack Review* 2 (Winter 1955) 2-3
16 *Ibid*. 19
17 Neil Compton, 'Coming of Age on Saint Urbain Street,' *Saturday Review* (July 1969) 38
18 Donald Cameron, *Conversations with Canadian Novelists* (Toronto 1973) 116
19 *Ibid*. 115

CHAPTER 13 Towards the Mystical Grotesque: *Beautiful Losers*

1 William Van O'Connor, *The Grotesque* 19
2 Leonard Cohen, *Beautiful Losers* (Toronto 1966)
3 Michael Harris, 'An Interview with Leonard Cohen,' *Duel* 1 (Winter 1969) 90-114
4 *Ibid*. 113
5 Norman O. Brown, *Love's Body* (New York: Random House 1966)
6 Sandra Djwa, 'Leonard Cohen: Black Romantic,' *Canadian Literature* 34 (Autumn 1967) 40
7 Harris, 'An Interview with Leonard Cohen' 107
8 *Ibid*.
9 Djwa, 'Leonard Cohen: Black Romantic' 39
10 Northrop Frye, *The Modern Century* (Toronto 1967) 84
11 *Ibid*. 84

CONCLUSION

1 *Survival* 173
2 J.M.S. Tomkins, introduction to *The Gothic Flame* xv
3 *Ibid*. xiii
4 Lawson, 'The Grotesque in Recent Southern Fiction' 171

Bibliography

PRIMARY SOURCES

Editions quoted in this study

Atwood, Margaret *Surfacing* Toronto 1972
Aubert de Gaspé, Philippe-Ignace-François *Le Chercheur de trésors ou L'Influence d'un livre*, with introduction by Léopold Leblanc. Montreal 1968
Blais, Marie-Claire *Mad Shadows* translation by Merloyd Lawrence, with introduction by Naïm Kattan. Toronto 1971
Carrier, Roch *La Guerre, Yes Sir!* translation by Sheila Fischman. Toronto 1970
Cohen, Leonard *Beautiful Losers* Toronto 1966
Hébert, Anne *Kamouraska* translation by Norman Shapiro. Toronto 1974
Kirby, William *The Golden Dog* with introduction by Derek Crawley. Toronto 1969
Ostenso, Martha *Wild Geese* with introduction by Carlyle King. Toronto 1961
Richardson, John *Wacousta, or, The Prophecy* with introduction by Carl F. Klinck. Toronto 1969
Richler, Mordecai *Cocksure* Toronto 1968
Tardivel, Jules-Paul *For My Country: Pour la patrie* translation by Sheila Fischman, with introduction by A.I. Silver. Toronto 1975
Watson, Sheila *The Double Hook* with introduction by John Grube. Toronto 1969

First editions

Atwood, Margaret *Surfacing* Toronto 1972
Aubert de Gaspé, Philippe-Ignace-François *L'Influence d'un livre* Quebec 1837

Blais, Marie-Claire *La Belle Bête* Paris and Quebec 1959
Carrier, Roch *La Guerre, Yes Sir!* Montreal 1968
Cohen, Leonard *Beautiful Losers* Toronto and New York 1966
Hébert, Anne *Kamouraska* Paris 1970
Kirby, William *The Golden Dog* Montreal 1877
Ostenso, Martha *Wild Geese* New York 1925
Richardson, John *Wacousta; or, A Tale of the Canadas* London and Edinburgh
   1833
Richler, Mordecai *Cocksure* Toronto and New York 1968
Tardivel, Jules-Paul *Pour la patrie: roman du XXe siècle* Montreal 1895
Watson, Sheila *The Double Hook* Toronto 1959

SECONDARY SOURCES

General background material: historical and critical

Books

Atwood, Margaret *Survival: A Thematic Guide to Canadian Literature* Toronto
   1972
Auerbach, Erich *Mimesis: The Representation of Reality in Western Literature*
   translated by Willard R. Trask. Princeton 1953
Barasch, Frances K. *The Grotesque: A Study in Meanings* The Hague 1971
Birkhead, Edith *The Tale of Terror: A Study of the Gothic Romance* London 1921
Clayborough, Arthur *The Grotesque in English Literature* Oxford 1965
Coleridge, Samuel Taylor *Lectures and Notes on Shakespeare and Other English
   Poets* London 1821. Collected and edited by T. Ashe. London 1900
Cook, Ramsay *The Maple Leaf Forever: Essays on Nationalism and Politics in
   Canada* Toronto 1971
Dandurand, abbé Albert *Le Roman canadien-français* Montreal 1937
Fiedler, Leslie A. *Love and Death in the American Novel* revised edition. New
   York 1969
Frye, Northrop *Anatomy of Criticism: Four Essays* Princeton 1957
Garneau, François-Xavier *Histoire du Canada* 5th edition. Paris 1920
Guthke, Karl *Modern Tragicomedy* New York 1966
Hassan, Ihab *Radical Innocence: The Contemporary American Novel* Princeton
   1961
Jones, D.G. *Butterfly on Rock: A Study of Themes and Images in Canadian
   Literature* Toronto 1970

Kayser, Wolfgang *The Grotesque in Art and Literature* translated by
   Ulrich Weisstein. New York 1966
Literary History of Canada: Canadian Literature in English general
   editor, Carl F. Klinck. Toronto 1965. Revised and enlarged edition
   1976
Malin, Irving *New American Gothic* Carbondale, Ill. 1962
Moss, John *Patterns of Isolation in English-Canadian Fiction* Toronto 1974
O'Connor, Flannery *Mystery and Manners* edited by Sally and Robert
   Fitzgerald. New York 1969
O'Connor, William Van *The Grotesque: An American Genre and Other Essays*
   Carbondale, Ill. 1962
Parkman, Frances *France and England in North America, 1855-1897*
   7 volumes. Boston 1893-1901
Richardson, John *The War of 1812* London 1842
Robertson, D.W., Jr *A Preface to Chaucer: Studies in Medieval Perspectives*
   Princeton 1969
Le Roman canadien-français: évolution, témoignages, bibliographie Montreal and
   Paris 1964
Ruskin, John *The Stones of Venice* 4 volumes, 1851-3. London 1906
Summers, Montague *The Gothic Quest: A History of the Gothic Novel* New
   York 1964
Sutherland, Ronald *Second Image: Comparative Studies in Quebec/Canadian
   Literature* Toronto 1971
Tougas, Gérard *History of French-Canadian Literature* 2nd edition, translation
   by Alta Lind Cook. Toronto 1966
Warwick, Jack *The Long Journey: Literary Themes of French Canada* Toronto
   1968
Wellek, René and Austin, Warren *Theory of Literature* 3rd edition. New York
   1962
Varma, Devendra P. *The Gothic Flame: A History of Gothic Novel in England*
   London 1957

Articles and chapters in books

Lawson, Lewis A. 'The Grotesque in Recent Southern Fiction' in *Patterns of
   Commitment in American Literature* edited by Marston LaFrance (Toronto
   1967) 105-79
Rigeault, Jean 'Le Conte au Québec' *Canadian Literature* 53 (Summer 1972)
   60-80

Other related works of fiction and poetry

Anderson, Sherwood *Winesburg, Ohio* New York 1947
Aubert de Gaspé, Philippe-Joseph *Les Anciens Canadiens* Quebec 1863
Carrier, Roch *Floralie, Where are You?* Montreal 1969
Casgrain, H.R. 'La Jongleuse,' *Les Soirées canadiens: recueil de littérature nationale* (Quebec 1861) 205-89
Contes et récits canadiens d'autrefois edited by Guy Boulizon. Montreal 1961
Doutre, Joseph *Les Fiancés de 1812* reprinted 1844. Montreal 1969
Faulkner, William *As I Lay Dying* New York 1930
Kroetsch, Robert *The Studhorse Man* Richmond Hill, Ontario 1970
Lemay, Pamphile *Les Vengeances* 3rd edition. Montreal 1930
McCullers, Carson *The Ballad of the Sad Café and Other Stories* reprinted 1951. New York 1958
Marmette, Joseph-Etienne-Eugène *François de Bienville*, 4th edition. Montreal 1924
O'Connor, Flannery *Three* New York 1968
Parker, Gilbert *The Seats of the Mighty* London 1896
– *When Valmonde Camer to Pontiac* Chicago 1895
Poe, Edgar Allen *Tales of the Grotesque and Arabesque.* 2 volumes. Philadelphia 1839
Taché, J.-C. *Forestiers et voyageurs: moeurs et légendes canadiennes* Montreal 1884

Critical material related to individual works analysed

Chapter 2 Canadian Prototype: *Wacousta*
Baker, Ray P. 'John Richardson and the Historical Romance' in *A History of English Canadian Literature to the Confederation* (Cambridge, Mass. 1920) 125-39
Moss, John *Patterns of Isolation in English Canadian Fiction* Toronto 1974
Pacey, Desmond 'A Colonial Romantic: Major John Richardson, Soldier and Novelist' Part I, *Canadian Literature* 2 (Autumn 1959) 20-31; Part II, *Canadian Literature* 3 (Winter 1960) 47-56
Riddell, William R. *John Richardson* Toronto 1926

Chapter 3 Decorative Gothic: *The Golden Dog*
Le Moine, James MacPherson *Maple Leaves: Canadian History, Literature* 6th series (Quebec 1894)
Pacey, Desmond *Creative Writing in Canada: A Short History of English Canadian Literature* revised edition (Toronto 1961) 74-8

Riddell, William R. *William Kirby* Toronto 1923

Sandwell, B.K. 'Debunking the Golden Dog' *Saturday Night* XL (4 October 1932) 2

Chapter 4 Towards the Grotesque: *Le Chercheur de trésors*

Dandurand, abbé Albert *Le Roman canadien-français* (Montreal 1937) 21-3, 33-4, 37-46

Hayne, David M. 'La Première Edition de notre premier roman' *Le Bulletin des recherches historiques* LIX (1953) 49-50

– 'Les Origines du roman canadien-français' *Le Roman canadien-français: évolution, témoignages, bibliographie* 46-50

Lacourcière, Luc 'Biographical Sketch of Philippe-Joseph Aubert de Gaspé' *Dictionary of Canadian Biography* X (Toronto 1972) 18-22

Marion, Séraphin 'Notre Premier Roman canadien-français' *Les Lettres canadiennes d'autrefois* IV (Ottawa 1943) 47-60

Chapter 5 Gothic Propaganda: *For My Country: Pour la patrie*

Barette, Victor 'Un Roman trop injustement oublié: *Pour la patrie*' *Le Droit* XVIII 28 (December 1931) 10

Hare, John Ellis 'Nationalism in French Canada and Tardivel's Novel *Pour la patrie*' *Culture* XXII (1961) 403-12

Chapter 7 Psychological Gothic: *Kamouraska*

Portier, Howard 'A Bloody Sleigh Driven by Desire,' *Globe Magazine* (October 1970) 35

Chapter 8 Sociological Gothic: *Wild Geese* and *Surfacing*

Grant, George *Technology and Empire: Perspectives on North America* Toronto 1969

Grosskurth, Phyllis 'Victimization or Survival' *Canadian Literature* 55 (Winter 1973) 108-10

Morley, Patricia 'Multiple Surfaces' *Journal of Canadian Fiction* 1 (Fall 1972) 99-100

Smith, Marion 'Period Pieces' *Canadian Literature* 10 (Autumn 1961) 72-7

Thomas, Clara 'Martha Ostenso's Trial of Strength' *Writers of the Prairies* edited by Donald G. Stephens (Vancouver 1973) 39-50

Chapter 9 Terrible Grotesque: *Mad Shadows*

Boivin, Gérard-Marie 'Le Monde étrange de Marie-Claire Blais, ou La Cage aux fauves' *Culture* 29 (March 1968) 3-17

Callaghan, Barry 'Interview with Marie-Claire Blais' *Tamarack Review* 37 (Autumn 1965) 29-34

La Marche, Jacques A. 'La Thématique de l'aliénation chez Marie-Claire Blais' *Cité Libre* XXX (juillet-aout 1966) 27-32

Marcel, Jean 'L'Univers magique de Marie-Claire Blais' *Action Nationale* LV (1965) 480-3

Wilson, Edmund *O Canada: An American's Notes on Canadian Culture* New York 1966

Chapter 10 Sportive Grotesque: *La Guerre, Yes Sir!*

Bailey, Nancy 'The Corriveau Wake: Carrier's Celebration of Life' *Journal of Canadian Fiction* 3 (Summer 1972) 43-7

Dionne, René 'La Guerre, Yes Sir!' *Relations* 331 (1968) 279-81

Faulkner, William *The Portable Faulkner* edited and introduced by Malcolm Cowley. New York 1967

Muscatine, Charles *Chaucer and the French Tradition* Berkeley 1969

Sutherland, Ronald 'Faulknerian Quebec' *Canadian Literature* 40 (1969) 85-6

Chapter 11 Symbolic Grotesque: *The Double Hook*

Monkman, Leslie 'Coyote as Trickster in *The Double Hook*' *Canadian Literature* 52 (Spring 1972) 70-6

Morris, Margaret 'The Elements Transcended' *Canadian Literature* 42 (Autumn 1969) 56-61

Chapter 12 Satiric Grotesque: *Cocksure*

Cameron, Donald *Conversations with Canadian Novelists* Toronto 1973

Cohen, Nathan 'A Conversation with Mordecai Richler' *Tamarack Review* 2 (Winter 1957) 6-23

– 'Heroes of the Richler View' *Tamarack Review* 6 (Winter 1958) 56-68

Compton, Neil 'Coming of Age on St Urbain Street' *Saturday Review* (July 1969) 36-8

Frye, Northrop *Anatomy of Criticism: Four Essays* New York 1969

Tallman, Warren 'Richler and the Faithless City' *Canadian Literature* 3 (Winter 1960) 62-4

– 'Wolf in the Snow' in *A Choice of Critics* edited by George Woodcock. Toronto 1966

Woodcock, George *Mordecai Richler* Toronto 1970

Worcester, David *The Art of Satire* New York 1960

Chapter 13 Towards the Mystical Grotesque: *Beautiful Losers*

Bowering, George 'Inside Leonard Cohen' *Canadian Literature* 33 (Summer 1967) 70-2

Brown, Norman O. *Love's Body* New York: Random House 1966

Djwa, Sandra 'Leonard Cohen: Black Romantic' *Canadian Literature* 34 (Autumn 1967) 32-43

Harris, Michael 'An Interview with Leonard Cohen' *Duel* 1 (Winter 1969) 90-114

Ondaatje, Michael *Leonard Cohen* Toronto 1970

Scobie, Stephen 'Magic, not Magicians' *Canadian Literature* 45 (Summer 1970) 56-60

Index